Soldiering for Freedom

How Things Worked

Robin Einhorn and Richard R. John, Series Editors

ALSO IN THE SERIES:
Sean Patrick Adams, *Home Fires: How Americans Kept Warm in the Nineteenth Century*

Ronald H. Bayor, *Encountering Ellis Island: How European Immigrants Entered America*

Soldiering for Freedom

*How the Union Army Recruited, Trained, and
Deployed the U.S. Colored Troops*

BOB LUKE & JOHN DAVID SMITH

Johns Hopkins University Press | *Baltimore*

Johns Hopkins University Press
2715 North Charles Street
Baltimore, Maryland 21218-4363
www.press.jhu.edu

Library of Congress Cataloging-in-Publication Data

Luke, Robert A., 1941–
    Soldiering for freedom : how the Union army recruited, trained, and
deployed the U.S. Colored Troops / Bob Luke and John David Smith.
        pages   cm. — (How things worked)
    Includes bibliographical references and index.
    ISBN 978-1-4214-1359-4 (hardcover : alk. paper) — ISBN 978-1-4214-1360-0
(pbk. : alk. paper) — ISBN 978-1-4214-1374-7 (electronic) — ISBN 1-4214-1359-0
(hardcover : alk. paper) — ISBN 1-4214-1360-4 (pbk. : alk. paper) — ISBN
1-4214-1374-4 (electronic) 1. United States—History—Civil War, 1861–1865—
Participation, African American. 2. United States. Colored Troops. 3. United
States. Army—African American troops—History—19th century. 4. African
American soldiers—History—19th century. I. Smith, John David, 1949–.
II. Title. III. Title: How the Union army recruited, trained, and deployed the
U.S. Colored Troops.
    E540.N3L85 2014
    973.7'415—dc23   2013040920

A catalog record for this book is available from the British Library.

*Special discounts are available for bulk purchases of this book. For
more information, please contact Special Sales at 410-516-6936 or
specialsales@press.jhu.edu.*

Johns Hopkins University Press uses environmentally friendly book
materials, including recycled text paper that is composed of at least
30 percent post-consumer waste, whenever possible.

In memory of my parents, Robert and Sally Luke—B.L.

For my dear friends, Nancy Mitchell and Stephen M. Wrinn—J.D.S.

CONTENTS

PREFACE

African Americans—slaves as well as freedmen—joined the Union army during the Civil War by the thousands. By war's end, two hundred thousand blacks had worn Union blue. About one-third of them died, several thousand in combat and the rest from wounds and disease. This volume describes how African Americans joined the army, how they made the transition from slave or civilian to soldier, and how they fought.

Many volunteered for service. Others were enlisted against their will. Few had held a gun, fired a shot, or knew how to read and write. They had to learn how. All served under the command of white officers, often a source of tension for both officer and soldier. Eager to prove themselves in battle, many found frustration in being assigned "fatigue duties," the grubby, boring chores that kept the army operating but offered no chance for glory. All encountered discrimination from white civilians—many of whom thought blacks would run from a fight at the first chance—as well as from white soldiers and officers.

We hope this book will help the reader understand how a variety of recruitment tactics, training methods, and battlefield events resulted in the rawest of recruits becoming professional soldiers who contributed significantly to the North's victory while winning the acclaim of many whites. African American soldiers faced more challenges than did white soldiers. This book tells you how they met them.

We wish to thank our editor, Robert J. Brugger, for asking us to write this book for the How Things Worked Series. Bob and his assistant, Melissa B. Solarz, provided valued assistance at every turn. We also thank J. Matthew Gallman for his insightful commentary on and critique of our manuscript and Gwendolyn L. Gill for her research assistance. Bob Luke thanks the staff at the Library of Congress, especially Thomas Mann, Anthony Mullan, and Sibyl Moses, for their help in finding sources; John Cuthberg at West Virginia

University for his research on the career of Major J. W. M. Appleton; Frank Smith and Hari Jones at the African American Civil War Museum for their guidance and support; and Judith E. Wentworth for her encouragement and forbearance. John David Smith thanks Leigh Robbins for her secretarial support and Sylvia A. Smith and Max for their patience and seemingly endless good cheer.

Soldiering for Freedom

Prologue

Twenty-five-year-old colonel Robert Gould Shaw called to attention the six hundred black soldiers of the Union's 54th Massachusetts Volunteer Regiment at dusk on July 18, 1863. The troops included a son of the popular black leader Frederick Douglass, Sergeant Major Lewis Douglass. Shaw descended from elite Boston abolitionists. His soldiers made ready to lead the northern army's assault on Fort Wagner, a Confederate stronghold on Morris Island, south of Charleston, South Carolina. If Fort Wagner fell, Union troops would then be positioned to lob shells into the venerable city, whose church spires one could see in the distance.

Shaw could understandably have declined Brigadier General George Crockett's invitation to lead the attack on Wagner. His men had just marched all day and all night under a blistering sun and a torrential rain. They had been without rations for two days and had not eaten since breakfast. Shaw knew, however, that if he accepted the invitation to lead the assault, the men of the 54th could demonstrate their valor to the vast majority of whites who, for various reasons, adamantly opposed the arming of blacks. Shaw sought to prove that African American soldiers possessed the same courage, fortitude, and fighting ability as white troops. He probably was unaware, however, that another Union commander, Brigadier General Truman Seymour, had boasted to his commander, Major General Quincy Adams Gillmore, that he could "run right over it [Fort Wagner]." In answer to Gillmore's question, "How?" Seymour replied, "Well, I guess we'll let Strong lead and put those damned niggers from Massachusetts in the advance; we might as well get rid of them one time as another."[1]

In spearheading the assault on Fort Wagner, the men of the 54th faced a daunting challenge. The Confederate bastion stretched across the entire neck of Morris Island, ruling out anything but a frontal attack. To prevent just such an assault, the Rebels had planted land mines in the sand over which an attack force would charge. Entrenched behind the walls of the fortress, the defenders possessed a clear view of the attackers.

The defenders had beaten back a previous Union attack. On July 10 Gillmore's white troops had successfully taken control of the southern end of Morris Island, leaving only the fort at the island's northern tip to be dealt with. On July 11 Gillmore sent three white regiments to take the fort. Of the 185 soldiers in the lead unit, only 88 made it back. The Confederates had held. Gillmore then ordered an artillery barrage on the fort that he thought would weaken its defenses enough for the next ground assault to take the fort with ease.

To ensure success, Gillmore positioned two white regiments, the 6th Connecticut and the 48th New York, directly behind the 54th to attack the fort's ocean side while the 54th hit its center. He ordered four other white regiments to stand ready. At 7:45 p.m., after calling his men to attention, Shaw ordered his troops to start the assault in "quick time" and then to move at "double quick" when they came within one hundred yards of the fort. The men triggered deadly land mines as they approached the enemy. At two hundred yards, Fort Wagner's three hundred defenders unleashed blistering fire on the men of the 54th Massachusetts with cannons and muskets. Shaw's men, now fewer in number but with no stop or pause, continued at the double quick. Many fell while crossing a water-filled trench directly in front of the fort. Reaching the top of the rampart that surrounded it, Shaw yelled, "Forward, Fifty-fourth!"[2] Soon after, a bullet pierced his heart.

As the regiment's surviving officers fired pistols at the Rebels, the men of the 54th Massachusetts broke into the fort and engaged the Confederates in hand-to-hand combat with musket butts and bayonets. The gray coats fought back in kind and with handspikes, gun-rammers, and swords. The larger-than-expected Rebel force and lack of promised support forced the black troops to back off the rampart, recross the ditch, and retreat back to the sand hills,

The celebrated attack of the 54th Massachusetts Volunteer Regiment on Fort Wagner, July 18, 1863. Fort Wagner protected the Atlantic approaches to Charleston, South Carolina, the seat of secession and site of the first shots of the war. Kurz and Allison Art Publishers of Chicago released this somewhat fanciful print and considered it suitable for framing and a place of respect in patriotic Union homes. Prints and Photographs Division, Library of Congress.

all the while taking causalities from rifle fire, grenades, and lighted shells. The 6th Connecticut and the 48th New York, having no more success than the 54th, joined in the retreat. Gillmore's remaining four regiments made a belated appearance and managed to breach the fort and engage in hand-to-hand combat with its defenders, but they also had to retreat and took heavy casualties. The three hours of combat that evening constituted a costly Union setback but established forever the indisputable fact that African Americans could fight with fortitude, valor, and courage.

The brief fight cost the 54th Massachusetts 3 officers killed and 9 wounded, 147 enlisted men known dead or wounded, and 100 missing—presumed dead or taken prisoner. In an act of blatant disrespect, Fort Wagner's Confederate defenders threw Shaw's body into a mass grave along with his fallen black comrades. Sergeant William Carney, wounded four times while keeping aloft the 54th's colors (the original color bearer had been killed), proudly carried the flag as he limped back into camp. For his actions, Carney received the Medal of Honor, first awarded by the U.S. government in July 1862.

Despite the failure of the attack to capture the Confederate fortress, the 54th's performance demonstrated the willingness, ability, and courage of African American troops to fight and to fight with valor. Many whites had predicted that the black man would cower in fear once engaged in combat and run scared if forced into battle. The year before, during a heated debate in the House of Representatives over arming former slaves, proslavery Kentucky congressman Charles A. Wickliffe declared that "a negro is afraid, by instinct or by nature, of a gun." "One shot of a cannon," Robert Mallory, another Kentucky legislator predicted, "would disperse thirty thousand of them."[3]

Though Shaw's troops had put the lie to those fallacious assertions, the hard fighting of the men of the 54th Massachusetts at Fort Wagner had little effect on the prevailing culture of segregation in the U.S. Army. Since passage of the Militia Act of 1792, custom dictated that only whites could serve as armed soldiers in federal forces. President Abraham Lincoln's final Emancipation Proclamation of January 1, 1863, authorized the use of African Americans as fighting troops, and the government organized them in segregated regiments.

Though segregated, the men of the United States Colored Troops (USCT) fought courageously alongside white units, effectively demonstrating the worth of African Americans as soldiers and men. Their presence in arms made clear that after 1863 Lincoln had transformed the war from a constitutional struggle over states' rights to a war of black liberation. By the end of the war, black troops comprised 133 infantry regiments, 4 independent companies, 7 cavalry regiments, 12 batteries of heavy artillery, and 10 batteries of light artillery. About 19 percent came from the eighteen northern states, 24 percent from the border states, and 57 percent from the eleven Rebel states. Black soldiers provided roughly ten percent of all Union troops. Though most whites had opposed the military mobilization of African Americans in 1861, circumstances changed so dramatically that in March 1865 four companies of the 45th USCT stood as part of the honor guard as Lincoln delivered his second inaugural address. A month later men from the 22nd USCT led the funeral procession that escorted Lincoln's dead body from the White House to the Capitol.

This book introduces readers to how Lincoln's administration came to recruit, train, and deploy about 180,000 black soldiers and 20,000 black sailors. Though the president promised blacks who wore the Union blue freedom and equal treatment, in practice they served a nation and military and naval forces rife with deep-seated racial prejudice. The book focuses on how the government mobilized and utilized blacks in battle and how white racism circumscribed and shaped their efforts. Ultimately blacks proved their mettle in battle, earned the gratitude of their country, and laid the foundation for African Americans' quest for true citizenship and freedom.

1 How Racism Impeded the Recruitment of Black Soldiers

THE CIVIL WAR offered northern free blacks and southern slaves profound opportunities to overcome proscription and segregation and to break free from the shackles of slavery, trading service in the Union army for respectability, equal treatment, and freedom. Though from the start of the war blacks eagerly sought to fight for President Lincoln's government, whites spurned their offers to serve. For the first two years of the internecine struggle most northerners—politicians, military officers, enlisted men, and the citizenry at large—opposed blacks serving on a par with whites in Union armies. Military service was a citizen's right. And the notorious *Dred Scott v. Sandford* (1857) case had determined that people of color were not citizens.

"No Colored Need Apply"

After Confederate forces fired on Fort Sumter in Charleston Harbor on April 12, 1861, to start the war, President Lincoln called for seventy-five thousand Union volunteers to suppress the southern rebellion. Lincoln intended that only whites could volunteer, however. The Militia Act of 1792 prohibited blacks from joining the army. The military was to be the province of whites, not blacks.

This is not to say, however, that blacks had not served under arms in previous wars. African Americans fought with the Continental army in the battles of the American Revolution even though General George Washington, upon taking command of the army in July 1775, decreed that no blacks should be enlisted and that those already in service should be mustered out. The resulting clamor of dissent from blacks who tried to enlist forced Washington to modify his decision within two months. African Americans already in the service could reenlist, but no new black recruits could be mustered in. For the rest of the war, except for a single Rhode Island regiment made up entirely of black soldiers, blacks fought alongside whites in integrated units— typically thirty to forty blacks per regiment. After independence, Congress followed Washington's opposition to employing blacks as armed soldiers in the new nation's armed forces. Only in the free states that abolished slavery during the war or immediately afterward did any of the five thousand blacks who had fought in the Continental army find freedom.[1]

The British enticed slaves to their side with promises of freedom for service. Thousands responded and joined white Loyalists in battles and skirmishes against Washington's forces. Their regiments carried names such as Ethiopian Regiment, Black Brigade, and Black Pioneers. Those fortunate enough to escape their masters' efforts to reclaim them after the war sailed from New York City on British warships to a challenging but free life on small, hardscrabble tracts of land in Nova Scotia. Over fifteen hundred settled in Shelburne.

Even though federal law banned blacks from serving in the army during the War of 1812, several states, notably New York, authorized the formation of black regiments to be led by white officers. A militia unit of free blacks, mostly veterans of the Haitian Revolution, served with General Andrew Jackson at the Battle of New Orleans in January 1815.

Once the Civil War began, attitudes as well as laws blocked black northerners from military service. Whites across the northern and border states interpreted the conflict as a white man's war; its sole purpose was to defeat the armies of the eleven seceded states and to restore the Union. A small minority of radical abolitionists, determined to abolish slavery immediately without compensating slaveholders, interpreted Lincoln's call for troops as the beginning of a war against slavery and for black military mobilization. But most northern whites opposed such policies. Few challenged the South's so-called peculiar institution, supported equal rights for blacks, or questioned white supremacy.

Free Negroes in the North composed only about 1.5 percent of the antebellum population. In Ohio, Pennsylvania, Indiana, Illinois, and New York, private institutions such as streetcar companies, theaters, and churches generally excluded black patrons, as did public institutions such as courts, militias, and schools. Freedmen could vote in much of New England and could vote in New York if they owned $250 worth of property. To be sure, a vibrant black middle class populated northern cities, but most black northerners typically worked in menial jobs as farmhands, hotel porters, barbers, coachmen, draymen (drivers of flatbed wagons), and waiters. Though Lincoln and his Republican colleagues opposed slavery's extension into the federal territories, neither in the elections of 1856 nor 1860 did they campaign on a platform to free the South's four million slaves or to confer citizenship rights on free blacks, north or south.

Despite being barred from service in the federal forces, thousands of northern blacks nonetheless offered their services to the Union in the spring 1861. They did so to help strike a blow against the enslavement of black southerners, to show their patriotism, and to make a case for equal treatment of blacks north of Dixie. Black northerners organized mass meetings, complete with bands and speakers, in Cleveland, Boston, New York, Detroit, Baltimore, and Washington, DC, demanding the opportunity to enlist. The "Negro waiter, cook, barber, bootblack, groom, porter and laborer stood ready at the enlisting office," exclaimed Joseph T. Wilson, who himself served in the 54th Massachusetts Volunteer Regiment.[2] A Philadelphia schoolteacher, Alfred M. Green, called on blacks in the Quaker City to forget "past grievances" and "take up the sword."[3] Three hundred men stepped forward. But Pennsylvania governor Andrew G. Curtin refused to enlist them in state forces.

Nicholas Biddle, a 65-year-old African American from Pottsville, Schuylkill County, Pennsylvania, was one of the first blacks to volunteer to fight the Confederates. A member of the Washington Artillery, a militia company composed of men from Allentown and Lehigh County, Biddle traveled to Washington, DC, on April 18, 1861, with his comrades to offer their services to President Lincoln's army. As the company marched through Baltimore to board trains at Camden Station en route to Washington, mobs of Rebel sympathizers attacked the northern volunteers. The sight of a black man in uniform incited the rioters, one of whom pelted Biddle in the head with a brick, knocking him to the ground and severely injuring him. Biddle thus may have been the first casualty of the war. Though prevented because of his race from joining the Union army as a soldier, Biddle served as an aide to Captain James Wren of the 48th Pennsylvania Infantry.[4]

In Ohio, in early 1862, the free black John Mercer Langston, a graduate of Oberlin College, offered to raise a regiment of black troops, but Governor David Tod declined his offer. Tod knew that blacks could not legally serve. Lincoln's first secretary of war, Simon Cameron, had made clear in the summer 1861 that his department had no plans to enlist blacks in the army. Many whites in Cincinnati had threatened violence if any black man was seen in Union blue within the Buckeye State. "This is a *white man's* government," Tod told Langston. "White men are able to defend and protect it," and "to enlist a negro soldier would be to drive every white man out of the service." Langston replied, "Governor, when you need us, send for us."[5] Similarly, Tod refused offers of military service from 115 black students at Wilberforce University.

Tod's counterpart in Connecticut held similar convictions. Governor William A. Buckingham, when faced with offers of service from his state's able-bodied black men, told them, "It seems to me that the time may yet come when a regiment of colored men may be profitably employed. But now, . . . it would create so much unpleasant feeling . . . that more evil than good would result."[6] In spite of the refusals, many Connecticut blacks donated money, horses, and food to the Union war effort.

Not only did legal barriers and racial prejudice work against the recruitment of black troops, but many, probably most whites, north and south, believed that blacks either could not fight or would refuse to fight if given the chance. Nineteen-year-old corporal Felix Brannigan of the 74th New York Volunteer Infantry expressed a common feeling toward black troops in the rawest language. "We don't want to fight side and side with the nigger," he wrote to his sister. "We think we are a too superior a race for that."[7] "We believe the colored folks desire to keep out of the way of cold steel," declared the *Brooklyn Daily Eagle*, "and we believe neither side will lose much by indulging them in this inclination."[8]

Coping with Whites' Fears and Prejudices

White southerners considered the idea of black soldiers both reprehensible and vexing. Southern slave owners and Confederate officials alike judged the war a white man's enterprise. "With us, all of the white race, however high or low, rich or poor, are equal in the eye of the law. Not so with the negro. Subordination is his place," declared Alexander H. Stephens, Jefferson Davis's vice president, in a speech delivered in Savannah, Georgia, on March 21, 1861.[9]

Two hundred years of the slaves' "subordination" had led many slave owners to hold erroneous beliefs about their slaves' character. Many masters, confusing behavior with innate characteristics, considered their slaves to be congenitally docile and childlike, lacking in ambition and initiative. Such behavior was almost predictable from people whom the law forbade to learn to read and write and who lived in fear of the lash, the noose, and the auctioneer's hammer. From the perspective of the master class, slavery ill-suited black men to the revered responsibilities and honor associated with and accorded the soldier. The very idea that a slave would have the courage, backbone, intelligence, and manners that white southerners associated with their ideal of a soldier, repulsed many. To arm blacks would be, in their view, a lie as well as a threat.

At the same time, realizing that bondage did not engender respect and affection, whites believed that blacks possessed a violent, beastly side, one that would vent itself against whites indiscriminately should slaves ever rise up or gain their freedom. Should the Confederates themselves arm the slaves, white southerners reasoned, they would put their very civilization at risk of black insurrection and debauchery.

Whites only had to look to the bloody history of slave revolts in the Western Hemisphere to justify such fears. In 1791 a massive slave rebellion in Haiti led to the deaths of four thousand French citizens, many of them gruesome. Slave revolutionaries nailed one man to a gate, cut off his arms and legs, and left him to die. Others tied a carpenter to two planks and sawed him in half. The leaders of the slave revolt carried the standard of a white baby's body impaled on a staff. Barbarities led to retaliation: French troops killed more than ten thousand slaves, executed another two thousand, and beheaded the revolt's spiritual leader, Dutty Boukman, burned his body, and thrust a pike through his head.

In early 1811, a group of about four hundred slaves outside of New Orleans armed themselves with knives, axes, and clubs and attacked plantations, killing two white men. Four hundred state militia and sixty federal troops gave chase. They killed sixty-six slaves upon apprehending them and sent sixteen to an unknown fate in New Orleans. Seventeen slaves went missing. Twenty years later, in August 1831, the slave preacher Nat Turner led seventy bondsmen on a two-day, twenty-mile armed rampage through Southampton County, Virginia. Turner and his band murdered at least fifty-seven white men, women, and children. Hundreds of soldiers from volunteer and militia companies responded by killing scores of blacks, some involved in the carnage and some not. The troops delivered Turner to the hangman. Images of insurrectionary slaves, whether in Haiti or the American South, came to haunt white southerners. Following the Turner revolt southerners tightened their slave codes, intensified their proslavery argument, and became aggressive in their defense of states' rights.

Masters and overseers responded to lesser acts of defiance with whippings and the sale of bondsmen and bondswomen to distant plantations. Faced with such harsh treatment and the specter of violent retaliation, most slaves adopted a posture of obedience and obsequiousness toward whites, masking their anger. Among themselves, however, slaves developed their own diverse culture, venting their feelings, singing African-inspired songs, sharing folk and communal traditions, and conducting religious services—more or less with their masters' permission. Much of this black cultural expression included symbolic and subtle acts of protest and resistance.

Once the Civil War broke out, slaves understood that the conflict might result in their freedom. Instinctively, many understood that they should run to the soldiers in blue, even if they did not know what would happen to them once they crossed Union lines. They comprehended that the enemy of their masters was their friend. In 1863, for example, a Louisiana slave informed a Union white officer: "Our masters may talk now all dey choose; but one ting's sartin,—*dey don't dare to try us.* Jess put de guns into our hans, and you'll soon see dat we not only know *how* to shoot, but *who* to shoot. *My* master wouldn't be wuff much ef I was a soldier."[10]

Two years earlier, in the summer 1861, when federal forces advanced on the railroad junction of Manassas, Virginia, slaves heard rumors of the impending campaign and tried to learn more of Yankee troop movements. They obtained much of their news by surreptitiously listening in on whites' conversations. After secession, Mary Boykin Chesnut, a now-famous diarist and the wife of South Carolina Senator James Chesnut Jr., insisted that her dinner guests converse in French. "We know," said one of her visitors, "the black waiters are all ears now, and we want to keep what we have to say dark."[11] In similar fashion, slaves alerted others on and off farms and plantations to the latest developments by talking in secret code. For example, a slave returning from town greeting a fellow slave might employ the phrase, "Good mornin', Sam, yo look mighty greasy this mornin'," meaning that he had information about prospects for freedom that he would share later on.[12]

As northern armies penetrated the South, Union forces worked their way up rivers and inland from the Atlantic and the Gulf, approaching and overtaking farms and plantations as they moved. The appearance of Union soldiers on farms and plantations bolstered the conviction of many slaves that their freedom would soon come. Many ran to Union lines to trade bondage for freedom, leaving their masters in the lurch. James Hervey Maury with his wife Lucinda Smith Maury owned and operated a 750-acre plantation, Nitta Tola, two miles from Port Gibson, Mississippi. "When the . . . enemy reached Nitta Tola," Maury later wrote, "the fetters of slavery were broken instantly and the hoe and plow handle dropped from the hands of the Negroes, and I ceased to be a planter forever. It is amazing with what intuitive familiarity the Negroes recognized the moment of deliverance."[13] Masters throughout the South were equally unaware of the determination of the bondsmen to be free.

The first slaves to escape farms and plantations—many with families in tow—who made their way to Union lines created a dilemma for federal military commanders. They lacked clear orders from their superiors as to how to respond to the sudden influx of black refugees. Some officers tried to return the slaves to their owners, believing it their duty to do so under the Fugitive Slave Acts of 1793 and 1850. Others, sympathetic to their plight, allowed the slaves to set up housekeeping on the camp's outskirts and put the men to work as laborers and the women as laundresses.

Nor did federal commanders know the legal status of the newly arrived blacks. Having escaped their masters' control, they were no longer technically enslaved, but they were not free in the eyes of the law. On May 23, 1861, little more than a month following the surrender of Fort Sumter, Major General Benjamin F. Butler, a former Massachusetts lawyer, Democratic politician, and then commander of Fortress Monroe, a federal military installation near Hampton, Virginia, took the matter of defining the status of fugitive slaves entering federal lines into his own hands.

The previous night, three runaway slaves had appeared at Fortress Monroe and sought protection from Butler, who obliged them. The following day Confederate major John B. Cary arrived under a flag of truce, demanding the trio's return under authority of the 1850 Fugitive Slave Act.

A Union newspaper artist gave a comical twist to a slave owner's anger and frustration as his human property ran off and thumbed his nose at his former master. Slaves needed little urging to leave their homes and seek freedom under the protection of Mr. Lincoln's soldiers. William A. Gladstone Collection of African American Photographs, Library of Congress.

Cary's demand put Butler in a bind. As a successful criminal attorney, Butler knew he could not allow his antislavery convictions to take precedence over the law. Thinking quickly, Butler informed Cary that he had no legal obligation to a foreign country, which Virginia, by its late act of secession, had allegedly become. Inasmuch as the Confederacy considered its slaves to be property, Butler reasoned, he could detain the three slaves as "contraband of war." Cary protested indignantly. Butler responded by offering to return the slaves if Cary's commanding officer would take an oath of loyalty to the Union. Cary departed the Union lines without the slaves. Butler's superiors in Washington, squeamish about labeling runaway slaves as freemen and thereby running the risk of alienating the border slave states as well as southern loyalist slaveholders, thenceforth applied the term "contraband" to slaves who absconded to Union lines. By defining absconding slaves as "contraband" or spoils of war, Butler argued, Union commanders did not need to return them to their former owners any more than captured livestock, cannon, or foodstuff. Lincoln's government quickly adopted Butler's "contraband of war" policy as its own.

Butler's strategy opened the gates to other Virginia slaves to flee their masters for Union lines and, over the course of the war, those from across the slaveholding South and the border slave states followed suit. Fifty-nine contrabands arrived at Fortress Monroe the following night, followed by hundreds more in the days and weeks to come. The fort became known among slaves as "Freedom's Fortress." Butler understood that arming the contrabands at Fortress Monroe would not only be illegal but would invite the displeasure of Lincoln and Secretary of War Edwin M. Stanton as well as criticism from the press. So he put the contrabands to work as laborers, cooks, laundresses, and servants to officers and in other forms of fatigue duty, a term used to describe noncombat duties ordinarily performed by soldiers.

In August 1861 Congress placed Butler's ad hoc policy into law when it passed the First Confiscation Act, authorizing the federal government to seize property, including slaves, belonging to Confederate insurgents. In March 1862 Congress further clarified the army's responsibility in the rendition of fugitive slaves when it passed an Article of War that prohibited the army from returning escaped slaves to disloyal masters, all but voiding the Fugitive Slave Acts of 1793 and 1850. And in the Second Confiscation Act of July 1862, Congress declared "forever free" Confederate-owned slaves who made their way to federal lines or who resided in rebellious territory that fell to federal forces. Significantly, the bill also authorized the president to utilize "persons of African descent" in any way that he considered "necessary and proper for the suppression of the rebellion." Another bill, the Militia Act of July 1862, gave Lincoln carte blanche in utilizing blacks in military roles, though the legislators clearly intended that the blacks serve as military laborers, thereby freeing white soldiers for combat roles. The bill also detailed the wages blacks employed by the U.S. military were to receive.

Several Generals Lend a Hand

The first blacks to bear arms for the Union Army did so under commanders who, unlike Butler, had no qualms in following their abolitionist persuasions despite the law, directives from Washington, and northern public opinion. These generals bucked the conventional racism in the country by not only recruiting and arming blacks but promising them their freedom as well. As early as August 1861, Major General John C. Frémont had incurred Lincoln's wrath when he unilaterally emancipated the slaves of Missouri Rebels, an action the president quickly rescinded. Undeterred by Frémont's experience, Major General David Hunter, a native Virginian and avowed abolitionist, took it upon himself to free and arm slaves in South Carolina during his tenure as commander of the Department of the South in the spring of 1862.

Union troops had seized and occupied South Carolina's Sea Islands (Port Royal, Lady's, and Saint Helena) off the coast of Beaufort in April 1862. Brigadier General Thomas W. Sherman had arrived there with Lincoln's authority to use the contrabands who flooded his lines in any capacity he wished but with the proviso that he not engage in a large-scale program of arming them. The Union plan for the Sea Islands combined military and missionary objectives, seizing and holding the strategically valuable territory while uplifting blacks who remained on the islands after their masters had fled to their mainland farms and plantations.

Much to the chagrin of abolitionists, General Sherman did nothing to disrupt the racial status quo along the South Carolina coast. He assured whites in Charleston that he would not tamper with their "peculiar institution." Massachusetts reformer Wendell Phillips bitterly protested Sherman's inaction. He pointed out that nothing in Lincoln's order precluded arming a limited number of blacks. War Department officials in Washington reassigned Sherman, deemed ineffectual, in March 1862.

His successor, General Hunter, asked Stanton if he could use his own discretion in emancipating and arming those loyal men he could find. As all whites had fled the islands, Hunter's intention to recruit and arm blacks could not have been clearer. When Stanton failed to reply to his query, Hunter presumed that Stanton would tacitly approve the equipment, uniforms, weapons, and pay necessary to transform the Sea Island blacks into Union soldiers. Accordingly, he ordered all able-bodied black men on the islands between the ages of 18 and 45 to report to Beaufort. White Union soldiers who opposed the project scared off many blacks by telling them that Hunter planned to position them in the front lines of every battle or that they would be sent to Cuba as slaves or be worked without pay. Some contrabands, abandoned by their former masters and working for pay on plantations under the control of Union-appointed superintendents, fled to nearby marshes and swamps to hide from heavy-handed Union recruiting parties. Using draconian tactics, Hunter's recruiters dragooned those slaves who remained from the fields, not even allowing them time to gather provisions from their cabins. As word of Hunter's impressment-gang tactics spread, more contrabands went to great lengths to avoid his recruiting officers. Their reluctance angered the abolitionist and successful businessman Gerrit Smith, who had supported John Brown's raid on the Union arsenal at Harpers Ferry, Virginia, in 1859, and who now donated liberally to efforts to recruit black troops.

These slaves lacked sufficient dedication to the cause of freedom, he complained. Colonel James Montgomery, an aide to Hunter and a recruiter of black troops who harbored no misgivings about impressing blacks who failed to volunteer, interpreted the same behavior differently. "By shirking the draft in every possible way; acting exactly like *white men* under similar circumstances," Montgomery said, "I conclude, they are undoubtedly *human*."[14]

Hunter soon found the contrabands more amenable to enlisting when, instead of coercion and threats, he offered them freedom. On May 9, 1862, again without authorization from Lincoln, the general declared martial law and issued a proclamation emancipating all blacks in the Department of the South, which encompassed South Carolina, Georgia, and Florida. Hunter also engaged a black Baptist preacher, the Reverend Abraham Murchison, who explained to the potential black recruits the political issues at stake and invited the men to enlist in Hunter's army. Many joined up.

Hunter soon gathered about eight hundred contrabands, whom he began to train. He established a board of officers, selected from his white units, to consider noncommissioned white officers who wished to rise in rank by becoming commissioned officers in the black regiment and appointed his nephew, Captain Arthur M. Kinzie, its colonel. Despite some success, Hunter's project of emancipating and arming blacks largely came to naught.

As in his response to Frémont's decree, on May 19 Lincoln summarily canceled Hunter's proclamation, while Stanton provided neither equipment to supply nor funds to pay his black enlistees. Lacking support from Washington, and recognizing his troops' low morale and high desertion rate, in August Hunter dismissed his regiment, save for what he considered his best company, which he maintained for guard duty on Saint Simons Island.

Though unsuccessful in raising and arming a black regiment in South Carolina, Hunter's efforts nonetheless positioned the questions of freeing and arming the slaves on the national stage. Newspapers had reported his every move. The *New York Times* thought white southerners might grudgingly submit to domination by the Union but never to their former slaves. To expect southerners to surrender to their slaves, the journalist reported, "armed by our Government and quartered in their midst, is an error, the folly of which is only exceeded by the devilish malignity that suggests it." The same reporter, foreseeing the possibility of blacks commanding whites, added that such an event would "excite the disgust of the country."[15] The *Boston Journal*, giving voice to a popular belief among whites, made the case that blacks found military service repugnant and would not "trade the cotton patch for the 'tented fields'" or the "bucolic hoe for the death-dealing musket."[16]

As reactions to Hunter's ill-fated recruitment and emancipation efforts continued to attract national media attention, a Vermont officer and ardent abolitionist, Brigadier General John W. Phelps, took it upon himself in the summer of 1862 to raise regiments of blacks from among the fugitive slaves who streamed into Camp Parapet in Carrollton, Louisiana, seven miles from New Orleans. Phelps's commanding officer, Benjamin F. Butler, who had been reassigned from Fortress Monroe to head the Department of the Gulf, angrily denied his request to arm the escaped slaves. "Phelps has gone crazy," Butler wrote his wife on August 2. "He is organizing the negroes into regiments and wants me to arm them. I told him he must set the negroes to work and not drill them."[17] Butler ordered Phelps to treat the blacks as contrabands, cutting timber and building fortifications. Protesting that he had no training in being a slave master, Phelps tendered his resignation, which Butler refused, prompting Phelps to return his commission directly to Lincoln.

Two weeks later, however, circumstances forced Butler to change his mind. Encouraged by Secretary of the Treasury Salmon P. Chase, and believing that the Confederates planned to attack New Orleans, Butler, unable to procure reinforcements from white commands, again conjured up a creative solution to a problem. He federalized the existing black Louisiana state militia units, the 1st, 2nd, and 3rd Louisiana Native Guards. Louisiana's Rebel government had originally accepted these regiments into its state militia in March 1862 as the Union navy advanced up the Mississippi and threatened New Orleans. The Guards consisted of freemen, many of them elite professionals, and at least one, Francis E. Dumas, was a slaveholder. Though the Confederates never seriously considered using the Native Guards in combat (the prospect of free blacks fighting for slavery and southern rights would have made excellent Rebel propaganda, however), Butler eagerly accepted the former black Confederates into federal service. He reasoned that activating a militia already formed but rendered inactive set no new policy, as Phelps had attempted to do.

While Butler federalized Louisiana militia units, the unauthorized recruiting of blacks also took place in Kansas under the leadership of Republican U.S. senator and brigadier general James H. "Jim" Lane, a Free-Soiler and radical abolitionist. Lane opened a recruiting office in Leavenworth, Kansas, in late August 1862. After complaints reached him about Lane's recruitment

Union troops at first tended to use former slaves for any drudge work they could avoid. In this drawing the Union army employs "contrabands," both men and women, to build a levee on the Mississippi River below Baton Rouge, Louisiana. Sketch by F. H. Schell, *Frank Leslie's Illustrated Newspaper*, May 9, 1863.

of blacks, Secretary of War Stanton telegraphed Lane, "You are not authorized to organize Indians, nor any but loyal white men."[18]

Like Hunter before him, Lane simply ignored Stanton's directive. He gave speeches to blacks throughout Kansas urging them to enlist. "We have been saying that you would fight," cried Lane, "and if you won't we will make you."[19] Lane placed notices in newspapers promising that each recruit would receive ten dollars a month plus subsistence and be mustered into the army as a regular soldier. He also pledged to issue certificates of freedom to those who had been slaves, as well as for their mothers, wives, and children.

Lane's promises, however, like Hunter's, lacked federal authority. He failed to mention that under the July 1862 Militia Act, three dollars of the black soldiers' monthly pay of ten dollars would be withheld as a clothing allowance. White troops received thirteen dollars a month, which included a three-dollar clothing allowance. The government also gave whites cash bounties, a bonus denied blacks. Congress had assumed, erroneously, that blacks serving in the military would be laborers, not armed soldiers, hence the discrepancies in pay. Even more serious, Lincoln had never authorized anyone in Kansas to issue freedom certificates. Undeterred, Lane nevertheless raised five companies—units that became the 1st Kansas Colored Volunteer Regiment. In October 1862 more than two hundred of his men skirmished with Confederate guerillas at Island Mound, in Bates County, Missouri, forcing the much larger Rebel force to retreat. Accounts of the engagement agreed that the black troops fought well. One newspaper reported "not a single coward among them" but noted that the black soldiers "were rather hard to handle and keep back, . . . like a pair of young, wellfed horses, anxious to go—and go at the guerillas!"[20]

Soon after Lane had commenced enlisting blacks in Kansas, recruitment of African American troops resumed in South Carolina, this time under Brigadier General Rufus Saxton, a West Pointer and Massachusetts abolitionist. In August 1862 Stanton, who had assigned Saxton to oversee abandoned plantations at Port Royal, authorized him to accept up to five thousand blacks as full-fledged Union soldiers. Though Lincoln publicly continued to oppose black enlistments, since June he had in fact been discussing the freeing and arming of slaves with members of his cabinet.

As Saxton began recruiting blacks, Lincoln decided to make public his decision to free the slaves. A few days after the bloody September 17, 1862, Battle of Antietam and the withdrawal of General Robert E. Lee's Confederate army from western Maryland, Lincoln judged that the Union, after suffering a series of military defeats, had achieved enough of a tactical victory to allow him to make public his momentous decision. The president feared that announcing his edict in the midst of military setbacks would make him look desperate. Accordingly, he issued the preliminary Emancipation Proclamation on September 22, promising to free slaves in those states "in rebellion against the United States" on January 1, 1863. Lincoln, acting as commander in chief, framed his decision as a necessary war measure. Although the preliminary Emancipation Proclamation made no mention of arming slaves (his final Emancipation Proclamation, issued January 1, 1863, did so), it nonetheless signaled a major redirection of Lincoln's position on slavery, a harbinger of the full-scale mobilization of African Americans as armed soldiers that occurred in 1863.

Meanwhile, Saxton, even with Stanton's approval to recruit blacks and Lincoln's preliminary Emancipation Proclamation, faced challenges enlisting black South Carolinians. Northern newspapers carried editorials decrying his efforts so soon after Hunter's recruitment attempts had failed. Blacks on the Sea Islands also retained bitter memories of Hunter's heavy-handed recruiting practices and his broken promises.

For example, as one of Saxton's recruiting sorties approached a large plantation, all but fifteen of the slaves managed to escape from their liberators. On the march back to camp, recruiters and their virtual prisoners came under enemy fire, ironically permitting the slaves turned recruits to bolt to freedom. Recaptured, they allegedly wept so loudly that the soldiers let them go. Other slaves went to great lengths to feign illness. Esther Hill Hawks, one of America's first woman doctors, had joined her husband, John, also a physician, as a Union medical officer in coastal South Carolina. She told of men who "hobbled" into physical examinations. These men, Dr. Hawks reported, arrived "with new sticks cut for the purpose not many rods from Camp" and complained of diseases that none of the doctors could understand. "The stubbornness with which they persist in shaming disease, in order to escape 'soldiering' is truly wonderful!" she said. "These examinations are very ludicrous."[21]

Frustrated, Saxton proposed appointing plantation superintendents, Union men who managed estates abandoned by their owners, as captains in return for their help in recruiting black troops. He hoped that their personal ties to the black laborers would prove helpful in enticing them to join the army. But black recruits only trickled in. Despite these setbacks, Saxton kept at it, and by November 1862 he had filled a regiment and had a full complement of white commissioned officers. Saxton selected the Harvard-educated abolitionist Thomas Wentworth Higginson to command the new unit, the 1st South Carolina Volunteer Regiment.

Higginson typified many non–West Point officers who commanded black troops in the early years of the war. A Unitarian minister in Newburyport, Massachusetts, Higginson prided himself on being one of the "Secret Six" who had funded John Brown's failed Harpers Ferry raid.

Higginson gained his military appointment by invitation, as did most commissioned officers of black troops before the War Department established the Bureau of Colored Troops in May 1863 and organized the USCT. He received a letter from Saxton while at dinner in Boston with fellow officers of the 51st Massachusetts Volunteer Regiment. Saxton's letter read in part, "My Dear Sir, . . . Your name has been spoken of, in connection with the command of this regiment, by some friends in whose judgment I have confidence. I take great pleasure in offering you the position of Colonel in it, and hope that you may be induced to accept."[22]

Higginson admired his African American soldiers, noting that they learned to drill and execute commands with greater ease than the white soldiers he had drilled in his Massachusetts regiment. Lenient with deserters, whom he could have brought before a firing squad, Higginson despaired of harsh punishment. In the case of one soldier who reappeared in camp after having been absent from duty without leave for five days, Higginson noted that "his clothes were in rags, and he was nearly starved, poor foolish fellow, so that we can almost dispense with further punishment. Severe penalties would be wasted on these people, accustomed as they have been to the most violent passions on the part of white men."[23] Other officers with similar sympathies who served under Higginson also came from the North, including Lieutenants Niles G. Parker (Massachusetts) and Henry A. Beach (New York).

Higginson, anxious to get on with the military business at hand, led his regiment on a series of raids into the coastal areas along the Georgia-Florida border in January 1863. Designed to destroy Rebel works and to bring back slave recruits, the first forays succeeded in spreading havoc among Confederates along the Saint Marys River. They cost the Rebels nine men killed and gained Higginson 150 recruits. The raids also illustrated the savvy of the slaves. During another raid, along South Carolina's Edisto River in July 1863, Higginson's gunboats reached a plantation shoreline. Hundreds of slaves of both sexes and all ages descended on the soldiers, hampering their attack on a Rebel battery atop a nearby bluff. Higginson later reported that an 88-year-old slave had described the plantation master's desperate plea and the slaves' response as follows: "De mas'r," Higginson reported the slave saying, "he stand and call, 'Run to de wood for hide! Yankee come, sell you to Cuba! run for hide!' . . . Ebry man he run . . . and ebry man run by him, straight to de boat."[24]

While the 1st South Carolina Volunteers conducted its raiding expeditions in January 1863, General Hunter resumed command of the Department of the South and began organizing a second black regiment, which became the 2nd South Carolina Volunteer Regiment. Perturbed that black recruits were slow to enlist voluntarily (Hunter believed that Sea Island blacks should willingly fight for the government that had liberated them), Hunter fell back on the strong-arm tactics that he had employed in 1862. Accordingly he conscripted all unemployed, able-bodied contrabands between the ages of 15 and 50, purposely leaving undefined the term "unemployed," thereby creating a thin line between conscription and kidnapping.

G. M. Wells, a plantation supervisor at a Mrs. Jenkins's plantation on Saint Helena Island, described to a congressional committee after the war how one of Hunter's sorties carried out his orders. In May 1863 four soldiers arrived, spent the night, and, following breakfast the next morning, discovered "nothing but horses and plows, without drivers, and idle hoes." The contrabands, according to an old man on the property, had "smelt a very large rat," and had repaired to the woods "to split rails." The soldiers rounded up all but two of the black men. When told why they would be taken away, the contrabands "seemed disheartened and sad, though none were stubborn or used harsh words. The soldiers used them very kindly and made no decided demonstration of authority." When the order to "march" was given, "a moaning and weeping such as touches the hearts of strong men burst forth." Wells reported that a woman told him "she had lost all her children and friends, and now her husband was taken and she must die uncared for."[25] Once the new unit formed, Hunter assigned the 2nd South Carolina Volunteers to the command of Colonel James Montgomery, who, like Higginson, led his black troops on successful raids against the Rebels in South Carolina, Georgia, and Florida.

Neither Higginson nor Montgomery knew their way among the many creeks, tributaries, and rivers that had to be navigated on these expeditions. For guidance they turned to many of their troops who lived in the area and, on one occasion, to Harriet Tubman, a runaway slave from Maryland who risked her life guiding other slaves to freedom. In June 1863 Tubman escorted Montgomery's 2nd South Carolina Volunteers on a raid up South Carolina's Combahee River. The raid resulted in the destruction of millions of dollars worth of commissary stores and cotton and netted an additional eight hundred recruits to Montgomery's force. Higginson's and Montgomery's raids provided skeptics yet more evidence that blacks would fight if given the proper training and opportunity.

Regardless how they joined Hunter's, Higginson's, or Montgomery's new regiments, after several months in uniform the black soldiers grew to take pride in themselves as soldiers and as men. One of the sergeants said about parading through Beaufort, South Carolina, behind a Marine band, "When dat band wheel in before us, and march on,—my God! I quit dis world altogeder." Another said, "We didn't look to de right nor to de leff. I didn't see notin' in Beaufort. Eb'ry step was worth a half a dollar."[26]

While Saxton and Hunter recruited blacks in South Carolina, in May 1863 Brigadier General Edward A. Wild, a Harvard-trained physician, abolitionist, and veteran of the Crimean War, undertook a similar mission in North Carolina. Accompanied by thirteen white officers, Wild raised the 1st North Carolina Colored Volunteer Regiment in New Bern from a population of freed slaves. Early in his recruiting efforts Wild relied on appeals to the freedmen's patriotism and promises of equality once the war ended. He found, however, that such promises failed to convince blacks to leave their steady-paying jobs and their loved ones to fight the Rebels. Trying a new tact, Wild engaged the assistance of the ex-slave brick-mason-turned-militant-abolitionist and Yankee spy Abraham H. Galloway and plantation supervisors to exhort men to enlist. Few rushed to the Union colors. Only when Wild changed his tactics, promising more concrete inducements, did his ranks begin to fill.

Wild guaranteed rations for the recruits and their families, schooling for their children, and a promise that, if captured by the Rebels, they would be treated humanely as prisoners of war. (This was a promise Wild could hardly expect to honor because in June 1863 the Confederates had announced their intention to kill or enslave all captured black soldiers and to execute their white officers as insurrectionists.) Wild also opened recruiting offices in the nearby towns of Plymouth and Washington, North Carolina, distributed recruiting posters around New Bern, and invited women to the recruitment meetings where many encouraged their husbands to sign up. "You's look a heap better in de crowd dar!" one woman told her husband, as she shoved him into the ranks.[27] Wild's successor, Colonel Alonzo G. Draper, a Boston lawyer who had organized a temperance society there and once led a strike of shoemakers, detailed several black noncommissioned officers to accompany him on recruiting trips. The uniformed African Americans served to convince potential slave recruits that they too could become black soldiers in blue.

Blacks in the Navy

From the beginning of the war the U.S. Navy faced problems similar to those that Butler had encountered at Fort Monroe, namely, what to do with the slaves who rowed, paddled, poled, or swam to Union vessels. Secretary of the Navy Gideon Welles gave them an answer. Believing that fugitive slaves then aboard Union ships could not be turned away, kept on board without working, or put to work without pay, on September 20, 1861, Welles conferred on them the rank of "boy," the Navy's lowest rank (today seaman recruit). He agreed to pay them ten dollars a month and provide one daily ration. Welles justified his actions on the precedent that since 1813 the navy had accepted free blacks into its service.

For the rest of the war naval officers encouraged the enlistment of contrabands who sought refuge on their ships; they sometimes employed accompanying women and children as cooks and laundresses. Naval officers did more than wait for blacks to approach them, however. They frequently sought out blacks in the form of "enlistment landings," such as the one led by Lieutenant G. B. Balch commanding the U.S.S. *Pocahontas*. Balch took the ship's surgeon ashore with him at Georgetown, South Carolina, on July 24, 1862. Dr. Reuben B. Rhoads returned to the ship with ninety-one new black recruits.

Prior to the war, the navy had limited the enlistment of blacks to 5 percent of its total force, messed and quartered black sailors with white sailors and, unlike the army, did not classify sailors by race. The sudden influx of black recruits, however, resulted in the maritime service exceeding the 5 percent figure. This led some commanders to segregate their crews on board ship. Rear Admiral David Dixon Porter, a Pennsylvanian and a member of one of America's most distinguished naval families, ordered blacks to be kept separate from white sailors aboard his ship, believing that blacks failed to maintain the most rudimentary levels of hygiene. Porter, convinced that whites were more susceptible to illness in hot weather than blacks, assigned blacks to perform all tasks to be performed on particularly hot days. Other commanders continued to mess and quarter black sailors with the rest of their crews. To do otherwise would have been to break with navy tradition and would have proven difficult given the limited space on board most ships. While accurate records remain elusive, in 1902 the Naval War Records Office reported that the 29,511 blacks who served in the Civil War navy amounted to one-fourth of all Civil War sailors. Black sailors suffered about 800 casualties, which accounted for a quarter of the 3,220 sailors killed, wounded, or taken prisoner during the war. Four African American sailors earned the Navy Medal of Honor.

Like the men of the USCT (who generally could not aspire to rise above the rank of sergeant), black sailors also faced limitations on how high they could advance in rank (the top rate available being seaman). Other ranks available to blacks included landsman, coal heaver, first- and second-class fireman, steward, and ordinary seaman. However, black sailors who knew the eddies and tributaries along the Confederacy's coastline could hold the position of pilot, comparable to the rank of a commissioned officer.

Lincoln Steps Forward

The sporadic efforts to recruit black soldiers prior to Lincoln's January 1, 1863, final Emancipation Proclamation produced limited results. Heavy Union casualties in 1862—at Shiloh in April, at the Seven Days in June, at Second Bull Run in August, and at Antietam in September—damaged the morale of white soldiers and civilians alike, making it more difficult for states to meet their military recruitment quotas. Lincoln came to realize that the southern insurgents would not, as he had initially hoped, surrender and that he thus urgently needed an infusion of new troops to squash the rebellion. Even so, worried about keeping the border slave states, especially Kentucky, in the Union, the president remained publicly cautious about putting multitudes of black men in blue uniforms. "To arm the negroes," he told an Indiana delegation on August 4, 1862, "would turn 50,000 bayonets from the loyal border states against us."[28] Six weeks later, just about the time Saxton received authorization to recruit black troops in South Carolina, Lincoln told another group of White House visitors, a delegation of Chicago Christians, "If we were to arm [the Negroes], I fear that in a few weeks the arms would be in the hands of the rebels."[29]

Yet military and political pressures to emancipate and arm African Americans continued to mount. In early 1862 Senator Charles Sumner of Massachusetts, himself a victim of proslavery violence in the Senate chamber in 1856 for his antislavery views, and then leader of Senate abolitionists, pleaded with Lincoln to "reconsecrate" the Fourth of July by freeing the slaves. He was no less eager to see freedmen enlisted in the Union army.

Despite his abhorrence of slavery, Lincoln hesitated in arming blacks because he knew that the U.S. Constitution, which he had taken an oath to protect, supported that institution. As the war progressed, however, Lincoln came to realize that the rebellion could bring down the Union and with it the Constitution itself. Were that to happen, Lincoln believed, he would not have been faithful to his constitutional duties. He therefore considered it imperative to take extreme measures that under normal circumstances would be unconstitutional in order to preserve the Union, which would in turn ensure the survival of the Constitution. Lincoln found himself confronted by the prospect "of either surrendering the Union, and with it, the Constitution, or of laying strong hand upon the colored element. I chose the latter," he wrote to a fellow Kentuckian.[30]

In a spirit of "indispensable necessity," on January 1, 1863, Lincoln issued the final Emancipation Proclamation, freeing the slaves, except those in the border states and in Union-controlled portions of the Confederate South. He soon welcomed slaves "into the armed services of the United States to garrison forts, positions, stations, and other places and to man vessels of all sorts in said service."

2 How Slaves and Freedmen Earned Their Brass Buttons

FOLLOWING THE ISSUANCE of the final Emancipation Proclamation on January 1, 1863, President Lincoln's government faced the challenge of recruiting, mustering, and organizing large numbers of African Americans into the federal military. Most of the recruits could neither read nor write, and few had ever fired a gun. Fewer still had any firsthand experience in combat. Beyond these disadvantages, many whites worked to stymie their mobilization and later military service, bitterly opposing the arming of blacks as symbolic of racial equality. The job of transforming slaves and free blacks into soldiers thus had to be done quickly. The Union's survival looked problematical at best in the first months of 1863.

Bringing Business to the Business of Recruiting

The federal government both drew upon previous methods and developed new techniques in enlisting the men who filled the ranks of what became the U.S. Colored Troops. It impressed blacks against their will, promised freedom and equality in return for voluntary military service, and engaged the help of clergy and newly recruited black soldiers to encourage enlistment. In its national recruiting campaign, Lincoln's administration drew upon congressmen, governors, mayors, and newspaper editors both to bolster its recruiting efforts and to raise money to finance recruitment activities. Prominent northern businessmen also contributed their organizing expertise and considerable wealth to the cause.

The best-known instance of businessmen recruiting black troops started at a January 1863 meeting of Massachusetts governor John A. Andrew and prominent abolitionists William Lloyd Garrison, Wendell Phillips, Julia Ward Howe, and Samuel Longfellow. The group gathered in Medford, Massachusetts, five miles north of Boston, at the Evergreens, the estate of George Luther Stearns. Proprietor of a manufacturing plant that produced sheet and pipe-lead, Stearns had been the primary financial backer of radical abolitionist John Brown's ill-fated October 1859 Harpers Ferry raid. Secretary of War Edwin M. Stanton authorized Andrew to recruit black soldiers for a Massachusetts regiment, providing that he not recruit in the Carolinas, where Generals Wild and Saxton already were at work. Knowing that Massachusetts's small free black population (fewer than ten thousand African Americans resided there in 1860) would not support a regiment of a thousand soldiers, Andrew and the abolitionists turned to Stearns, a successful businessman, for help.

Stearns had a knack for managing large groups of people and set to work immediately forming what he termed the Black Committee. Composed of fellow businessmen including Amos A. Lawrence, owner of Ipswich Mills, the largest producer of knit goods in the country, and Richard Hallowell, a prominent wool merchant, the men anted up $500 each to underwrite their recruitment efforts. Stearns eventually expanded the committee to one hundred members. The men placed advertisements in more than one hundred newspapers and raised over $100,000. Some newspapers not only carried recruitment advertisements but collected contributions as well. The *Chicago Tribune*, for instance, volunteered the services of one its employees, Alfred Cowles, to help organize the 1st Regiment of Illinois Volunteers (Colored) in January 1864. The *Tribune* listed the names of donors and the amount of each contribution to encourage "our substantial men [to] at once furnish the means to complete the organization of the 'First Regiment of Illinois Colored Volunteers.'"[1]

Stearns expanded the committee's reach by establishing a network of influential black agents, each responsible for setting up and supervising recruiting in a particular state. Recruiters fanned out to the Mississippi valley, as far west as Saint Louis, throughout the northern states, and into Canada, where they gave speeches; went door to door; frequented barbershops, pool halls, and churches; and called on stores and businesses of all types and sizes in search of black recruits. Stearns paid them a commission of two dollars for each recruit. The recruiters included the black abolitionist and editor Frederick Douglass, the black writer and orator William Wells Brown, the black abolitionist and lawyer John Mercer Langston, the distinguished black clergyman Henry Highland Garnet, and Martin R. Delany, a black physician, African explorer, black nationalist, and U.S. Army officer. In 1865 Delany became the first black officer commissioned as a major, the highest rank attained by a black soldier at the time. Though he never served in combat, Delany nonetheless successfully recruited for the USCT and, following the war, served with the Freedmen's Bureau.

Stearns also recruited actively. Along with his son Frank and a physician, who examined volunteers prior to their being accepted for service, the three men first went to Rochester, New York, in late February 1863 and then to Toronto, Canada, and back to Buffalo, New York. They netted 120 recruits on this trip alone. Not one to shy away from telling people what he knew they wanted to hear, Stearns, following an impassioned speech about the benefits of volunteering at a town meeting in Buffalo, answered a question about blacks becoming line officers. Without authority from anyone in Lincoln's administration, Stearns assured his audience that bias against men of color serving as officers would soon change and, accordingly, that blacks would be receiving commissions as officers within six months. Replying to a question about providing for recruits' families, Stearns, again without authorization, promised to ensure that the government would provide for recruits' family members. With such assurance twelve men stepped forward. By March 24, 1863, another thirty had signed on.

While Stearns and his agents recruited black soldiers across the North, Governor Andrew, despite his state's limited black population, was determined that Massachusetts would sponsor a black regiment. Accordingly, he commissioned J. W. M. Appleton as second lieutenant in the new 54th Massachusetts Volunteer Regiment, charging him with recruiting a company of African American troops. Appleton, a Boston abolitionist, opened an office on Cambridge Street in February 1863 and by early March had recruited enough men from the Boston area to form Company A of the 54th Massachusetts. Andrew then relieved Appleton of his recruiting duties, promoted him to captain, and placed him in charge of drilling Company A at the 54th's Camp Meigs in Readville, Massachusetts, near Boston.

On their way to Camp Meigs, Stearns's recruits, who also came to join the 54th Massachusetts, passed through pockets of strong anti–African American sentiment in Ohio and New York. Aware that possible violence might be directed at the black recruits, Stearns avoided gatherings of unruly crowds on departure day. He arranged for white recruiters to purchase railroad tickets for the men so that their departure would not be known until the last minute. Stearns made sure that all recruits traveled to Boston on the Erie Railroad. Its conductors supported his work, and the new soldiers would have to make but one transfer, thereby limiting their possible exposure to anti-black white mobs.

Stearns enjoyed his work. He told Governor Andrew in April 1863, "This work is popular among all classes. The Republicans want them to go to the war and the rest of the people because they want to get rid of them. If the President would conscript them, men, women and children, and take them south he would be so popular that it would insure his election for the coming term."[2]

Back in Boston, Appleton encountered his own share of white racism. He reported that "I had been told by Copperhead friends that I was a d——d fool,— that the slave drivers would 'come out & crack their whips,' and the niggers would run, & I be butchered and many other things had come to us showing a lack of sympathy, to say the least, with our enterprise."[3]

In spite of such prejudice, the ranks of the 54th Massachusetts Volunteers filled by the end of March 1863. The men of the 54th, most of whom were free-born blacks, hailed from twenty-eight states, the District of Columbia, and Canada. Pennsylvania supplied the most men, 212, followed by New York with 133, Massachusetts with 122, Virginia with 73, and Ohio with 52. Another regiment, the 55th Massachusetts Volunteer Regiment, soon after also mustered into service. Its composition demonstrated much the same reach of Stearns's recruiting network as that seen in the 54th: 80 percent of its men came from Ohio, Pennsylvania, Virginia, Indiana, Kentucky, Missouri, and Illinois. The remainder of the recruits hailed from eighteen other states plus the District of Columbia and Canada. Two-thirds of the recruits registered their occupation as farmer or laborer. According to their commander, Colonel Norwood P. Hallowell, most of the men were "poor and ragged" when they entered Camp Meigs.[4]

The 54th Massachusetts not only constituted the first black regiment recruited in the North, and one of the first to be organized with the backing of Lincoln and Stanton, but it also became one of the most famous African American fighting forces, gaining considerable fame from the 1989 movie *Glory*. Taking considerable historical license, the film dramatized the regiment's history down to its bloody and unsuccessful charge against Confederate forces at Fort Wagner, near Charleston, South Carolina, on July 18, 1863.

The movie's portrayal of the selection of Robert Gould Shaw, son of a wealthy Boston abolitionist, by Governor Andrew as the regiment's colonel did accurately identify the principals but failed to show that Shaw declined Andrew's initial offer. "If I had taken it," Shaw explained in a letter to his sister Annie, "it would only have been from a sense of duty; for it would have been anything but an agreeable task."[5] Subsequently, he changed his mind.

Like many white officers of the USCT, Shaw—who had served as lieutenant and then captain in the 2nd Massachusetts Volunteers before being wounded at Antietam in September 1862—had little prior direct contact with people of color. Not surprisingly, he displayed some of the racial prejudices of his day. For example, Shaw early on called himself a "Nigger Col." and referred to the first black recruits he met in February 1863 at Camp Meigs as "darks" and "nigs." Like those of other white officers, however, Shaw's attitude toward and understanding of black soldiers became more positive as he came to know them. Within weeks he referred to the recruits as men, explaining to his mother, "Everything goes on prosperously. The intelligence of the men is a great surprise to me. They learn all the details of guard duty and Camp service, infinitely more readily than the Irish I have had under my command."[6]

Shaw's early work with Massachusetts's two African American regiments pleased Andrew, who, aware of the public's sensitivity toward arming blacks, nevertheless pressed Stanton to commit the 54th Massachusetts to combat as soon as possible. "Our Fifty-fourth is being raised and officered for *active* not *fatigue* duty," Andrew wrote Stanton in April. He asked Stanton to dispatch the 54th to coastal South Carolina, where the fighting would allow the troops "a place in onward and honorable movements in active war."[7] Major General John G. Foster, commander of the 18th Army Corps stationed in New Bern,

North Carolina, also requested that the secretary of war send the 54th to South Carolina but for a different reason. "White troops are very liable to the malarious influences of the climate, which of course negro troops can stand," Foster explained in early May.[8] Stanton, without disclosing his reason for doing so, sent Shaw's men to South Carolina. There they achieved an honorable place both in the war and in American historical memory.

On May 28 the 54th left Boston for South Carolina amid cheers, tears, and sneers. Governor Andrew reviewed the troops on the Boston Commons. Aboard the steamer *De Molay* a few days later, Shaw wrote, "The more I think of the passage of the Fifty-fourth through Boston, the more wonderful it seems to me. Just remember our own doubts and fears, and other people's sneering and pitying remarks, when we began last winter, and then look at the perfect triumph of last Thursday."[9] Appleton noted in his diary: "We paraded on the Common & marched through many streets amid blessings, shouts, & some tears,—strangers clasped our hands, & blessed us."[10]

Other Bostonians reacted differently, offering disapproval, not blessings. For example, members of the Somerset Club stuck their heads out of windows and hissed as the soldiers passed by. An editorial in the Irish community newspaper, the *Boston Pilot*, declared, "They are as fit to be soldiers of this country, as their abettors [the abolitionists] are to be its statesmen. One Southern regiment of white men would put twenty regiments of them to flight in half an hour. *Twenty thousand negroes on the march would be smelled ten miles distant. . . .* There is not an American living that should not blush at the plan of making such a race the defenders of the national fame and power."[11]

Several of Lincoln's high-ranking officers shared the sentiments expressed by the *Pilot's* editor. Brigadier General Thomas G. Stevenson, a Boston native, let it be known from his camp in South Carolina that he would prefer that the South win the war rather than the Union win with the help of black troops. General David Hunter arrested Stevenson for what he considered his treasonous statements. In 1864 Colonel Frank Wolford, a Kentuckian who organized a white cavalry unit, gave speeches throughout the commonwealth condemning the use of African American soldiers in particular and Lincoln's presidency in general. Military officers arrested him twice. Both times Lincoln paroled him.

Frederick Douglass, on the other hand, who had long criticized Lincoln for moving too slowly in enlisting men of color, praised Lincoln's actions.

The black abolitionist predicted that the arming of black troops would transform African Americans, denied equal rights for two centuries, into American citizens. "Once let the black man get upon his person the brass letters, U.S.; let him get an eagle on his button, and a musket on his shoulder, and bullets in his pocket, and there is no power on the earth or under the earth which can deny that he has earned the right of citizenship in the United States," Douglass informed a wildly cheering audience at Philadelphia's National Hall on July 6, 1863.[12]

Freed Slaves Overwhelm Union Lines

While Stearns and recruiters across the North continued their work, the number of fugitive slaves who appeared at Union army camps in the South mushroomed. Even though Congress had earlier passed confiscation legislation prohibiting commanders from returning slaves to farms and plantations and granting freedom to those who reached Union lines, some Union commanders nonetheless remained uncertain how to treat slave refugees. Were they slaves, federal property, or citizens? Should they labor or soldier?

Because of their ambiguous status, some federal officers kept the contrabands in camp, while others tried to return them from whence they came. From Helena, Arkansas, in January 1863 Colonel Cyrus Bussey sought guidance from Major General Samuel R. Curtis, commander of the Department of Missouri. "There are a great many Negro men, women and children coming into our lines," Bussey wrote Curtis. "Would be pleased to receive some instructions from you."[13] Curtis passed Bussey's request up the line to Major General Benjamin M. Prentiss, who in turn referred the matter to Major General Henry W. Halleck, Lincoln's general in chief. On March 31 Halleck advised Major General Ulysses S. Grant, then commanding the Army of the Tennessee, that every Union officer must, in accordance with the final Emancipation Proclamation, "cheerfully and honestly endeavor to carry out the measures so adopted."[14] Those measures included putting all able-bodied blacks to work, if not as soldiers, then as laborers, cooks, and teamsters. Such policy would bolster Union forces and deprive the Confederates of badly needed labor. Grant assured Halleck that he would so instruct his officers. Bussey and Curtis now had their marching orders.

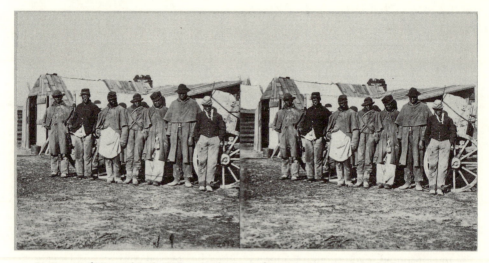

"A Group of 'Contrabands.'" Former slaves performed many menial jobs for the army, including that of teamster—driving teams of horses, mules, and oxen. These teamsters were stationed at Cobb Hill, Virginia. Photograph by John C. Taylor, Hartford, Connecticut. William A. Gladstone Collection of African American Photographs, Library of Congress.

Lorenzo Thomas Picks Up the Pace

Meanwhile Secretary of War Stanton ordered Adjutant General Lorenzo Thomas to launch a systematic drive to recruit blacks throughout the Mississippi valley, from Cairo, Illinois, to Vicksburg, Mississippi. A career officer with extensive administrative experience, Thomas began his new assignment (some said that Stanton had banished him to the Mississippi valley to remove him from Washington) with wide latitude but without the war secretary's full confidence. Stanton neither trusted nor liked Thomas, having frequently dispatched him on assignments to various unimportant posts. The secretary of war no doubt considered his assignment of Thomas to recruit blacks in the Mississippi hinterland in the same spirit. Thomas nevertheless left Washington with Stanton's full authorization not only to enlist African Americans but to appoint officers to lead them as well.

Thomas began his work on March 30 at Cairo, where he found fifteen hundred destitute blacks—men, women, and children—in cramped quarters suffering from malnutrition, smallpox, measles, and pneumonia. Thomas first mustered all able-bodied males into the army. Next, knowing that returning women, children, and the infirmed to their masters would subject them to violence, he assigned blacks unfit for combat but fit for work to till land for pay on abandoned and confiscated plantations and provided humanitarian care for the sick and aged. Slave refugee Richard Glover, who arrived at Cairo without his family, learned that his ex-master beat his wife regularly with a buggy whip. Another former slave, Wilson, received word after enlisting that his master forced his son to work through the winter and spring without shoes, knocked his daughter down, kicked her while on the ground, and subjected all family members to verbal abuse. Clearly Thomas and the War Department would have to develop procedures not only for recruiting black troops but also to accommodate, care for, and protect their families from slaveholders, Confederate forces, and guerillas.

As he proceeded down the valley, Thomas spoke eloquently and forcefully to crowds of refugee slaves, often numbering in the thousands. For example, on a recruiting stop in Memphis on May 21, he admitted that he had owned slaves, had been nursed by slaves, and had often observed slaves at work but insisted that he was now fully committed to emancipation. In clear and direct terms Thomas told the recently freed bondsmen and women what Lincoln's government considered the benefits and responsibilities of their freedom. Freed people were not to sit around but to work either on leased plantations or as soldiers. "President Lincoln," Thomas lectured the crowd, "has set you free—will you fight? . . . Suppose I would give you guns, and you should see a party of guerrillas in the woods, what would you do?" "Fotch 'em all in, Massa Thomas," roared the freedmen and women in unison. Feeling the energy of the crowd, Thomas implored them to sing. A *New York Times* reporter described the scene: "To us it looked like a camp-meeting. . . . My heart was surged with emotions."[15]

In another recruiting pitch, this one at Goodrich Landing, Louisiana, on November 28, Thomas invoked the Lord, to three thousand blacks and whites dressed in their Sunday best. "Providence," Thomas said, "has decreed that the black men of the country should be soldiers." The job of officers, Thomas made clear, was to "elevate and improve their minds," and planters, he thundered from his pulpit, were now to be as concerned with the "good of the negroes," as they were with profits.[16]

Not surprisingly, Thomas encountered racism at every stop on his recruiting tour, and he confronted it head on. The general reminded all listeners of Lincoln's determination to use black soldiers to help restore the Union.

"I come from Washington," Thomas informed white Union troops at Lake Providence, Louisiana, on April 18, 1863, "clothed with the fullest power in this matter. . . . I can act as if the President of the United States were himself present," he told the troops. "I am directed to refer nothing to Washington, but to act promptly—what I have to do, to do at once—to strike down the unworthy and to elevate the deserving." If any commanders still wondered what to do with former slaves in their camps, Thomas explained, "They are to be received with open arms; they are to be fed and clothed; they are to be armed."[17]

Thomas warned that any soldier who deserted in opposition to serving with blacks would be shot for treason. Any soldier who interfered with the recruitment of African American troops would be court-martialed. Any soldier who mistreated a member of the USCT would be cashiered from the service. In one case, in August 1863, William Yokum, in charge of contrabands at the federal garrison at Cairo, kidnapped Morris McComb, a former slave employed by the quartermaster. Yokum sold McComb for fifty dollars to Joseph K. Gant, who in turn enslaved McComb in Kentucky, a border state exempt from the final Emancipation Proclamation. For his crime, a military tribunal sentenced Yokum to five years at hard labor at the penitentiary in Albany, New York.[18]

By mid-1863 Union commanders routinely welcomed fugitive slaves who arrived at their posts voluntarily. Thomas also authorized federal troops to "gather" black recruits when foraging for Rebels, foodstuff, and livestock. Because Thomas gave no explicit instructions on how to "gather" black recruits, many officers brought blacks to induction camps against their will. In February 1865, for example, complaints reached Washington that federal recruiters around Henderson, Kentucky, were coercing blacks to join the USCT. Lieutenant Colonel John Glenn of the 120th USCT reportedly was "forcing negroes into the Military service, and even torturing them—riding them on rails and the like—to extort their consent." President Lincoln ordered Glenn not to impress black recruits into the service any more than white recruits. He also instructed Secretary of War Stanton to investigate accusations that recruiting officers in Maysville, Kentucky, were also coercing blacks into the military.[19] Thomas soon ordered an end to the use of force and authorized white civilians to raise black regiments. Thomas next commissioned the recruiters as officers in the regiments.

In addition to seeking recruits from the Mississippi valley, Thomas's agents attempted to recruit blacks already in the service but consigned to fatigue duty to serve as soldiers. Major General William T. Sherman resented recruiting agents interfering with black laborers who worked under his command. In September 1864 Sherman complained against both emancipation and black recruitment. "I dont see why we cant have some sense about negros," Sherman complained, "as well as about horses mules, iron, copper &c.—but Say nigger in the U.S. and . . . the whole country goes Crazy. . . . I like niggers *well enough* as niggers, but when fools & idiots try & make niggers better than ourselves I have an opinion."[20] Sherman ordered all recruiting of blacks within his command to stop and threatened to imprison those who continued the practice. Thomas lost this battle.

Sherman's rebuff of Thomas's agents represented a rare setback for the recruiter, however. As 1863 drew to a close, he had mustered in close to 27,000 black troops. By the end of 1864 that number had grown to 72,000. He also successfully maintained the strength of his black regiments at approximately a thousand men and continued to provide care for soldiers' families, fought against black soldiers doing more than their share of fatigue duty, and discharged officers he deemed careless or indifferent to commanding black troops.

Thomas's success inspired Major General Nathaniel P. Banks, a former governor of Massachusetts who had replaced Butler as commander of the Department of the Gulf, to raise twenty-one regiments that Banks designated the Corps d'Afrique. Banks had an easier task than either Thomas or Stearns in enlisting African American soldiers. In June 1863 he commandeered the regiments already being raised by Brigadier General Daniel Ullmann, a former New York City prosecutor whom Lincoln had sent to Louisiana to raise black regiments, into his Corps d'Afrique. Banks also integrated the Louisiana Native Guards, the militia regiments that Butler had federalized in New Orleans in 1862, into his new corps. Banks then turned to conscripting as many black recruits as he could find in order to fill the ranks of his regiments by August.

The 9th Regiment Corps d'Afrique (later renumbered the 81st USCT) was one of the units Ullmann recruited in Louisiana. In April 1864 a white officer from the 81st reported to Maine's *Bangor Daily Whig and Courier* that "a few days since we had had two colors presented to us, and the Regt formed a square, and every man and every officer got down on his knees and swore— so help him God—those colors never be taken from us,—and I believe they never will be. Every man said he would die by them. I never saw troops that wanted to get into a fight quite as much as they do. You will hear a good account of us when we do go in." For all their determination to enter combat, however, the men of the 81st, like many of the USCT regiments, performed garrison duty and fatigue labor for their entire term of service.[21]

Centralizing the Recruitment Process

The surge in black troops in 1863 overwhelmed the Adjutant General's Office, the division within the War Department that provided administrative support to commanders in the field. To facilitate the establishment and mobilization of black soldiers, in May 1863 Secretary of War Stanton created, within the Adjutant General's Office, the Bureau of Colored Troops (BCT), to provide direction and coordination to the army's efforts to recruit African Americans. This branch of the War Department moved quickly to systematize black units already organized to oversee the enlistment of new units, and to establish procedures to identify and train white commissioned officers for black regiments.

Stanton appointed Major Charles W. Foster to head the new bureau, with the title of assistant adjutant general. In one of his most controversial actions, for most units Foster replaced numbered state designations (such as the 127th Ohio Volunteer Infantry) with numbered federal designations (the 5th USCT) in the newly formed USCT.

This numbering system not only served to distinguish black from white regiments, both of which had carried state names in their designations, but made clear that the black units served under federal auspices, not state authority. The 1st South Carolina Volunteers thus became the 33rd USCT. The 1st Louisiana Native Guards became the 73rd USCT. The 1st Arkansas Volunteers of African Descent morphed into the 46th USCT. Only a handful of units, including the 54th and 55th Massachusetts Volunteer Regiments, the 5th Massachusetts Colored Cavalry, the 29th Connecticut Infantry, and the 14th Rhode Island Heavy Artillery, retained their state designations. Colonel Higginson considered the change in designation "a most vague and heartless baptism." It dispirited his recruits, who were proud that their regiment's name included the words "'de Fus' Souf."[22] White regiments retained their numbered state names.

At about the time that Stanton created the BCT, he learned of Stearns's recruiting successes. His businesslike recruiting methods impressed the secretary of war, who invited him to Washington and offered the industrialist the position of assistant adjutant general with a commission as major, the title of recruiting commissioner for the USCT, and $5,000 in government funds. Stearns accepted the new position and established headquarters in Philadelphia in June 1863. He worked closely with the BCT but reported directly to Stanton.

On June 22 Stanton ordered Stearns to raise three regiments of black troops in Philadelphia under the following conditions: The troops would serve for three years or the duration of the war. Unlike white recruits, the men would receive no bounties. And unlike white troops, who received thirteen dollars per month that included a three-dollar clothing allowance, as per the Militia Act of July 1862, the blacks would be paid ten dollars a month, three dollars of which would be deducted as a clothing allowance. Philadelphia's sixty-member Supervisory Committee for Recruiting Colored Regiments, composed of businessmen sympathetic to the causes of emancipation and black uplift, helped Stearns in his recruiting efforts. It raised money, distributed circulars, held rallies, and fed and transported recruits to Camp William Penn for training.

To help mobilize black recruits, the Supervisory Committee published a two-sided handbill that captured the symbolism of military emancipation during the war. One side of the handbill contained a recruiting poster calling blacks to arms, to free their slave brethren, to reunite the nation, and to stand as equals with whites. The poster reads: "All slaves were made Freemen by Abraham Lincoln, President of the United States, January 1st, 1863. Come, then, able-bodied Colored Men, to the nearest United States Camp, and fight for the Stars and Stripes." The reverse side of the poster is a richly colored lithograph of an African American officer with shoulder straps and dress sash at the center of the print, glancing toward the heavens. Other blacks—soldiers, slaves, and presumably freedmen—surround the USCT officer.[23]

Camp William Penn, located in Chelten Hills, twelve miles north of Philadelphia, sat on land adjacent to that owned by Lucretia Mott, the famous abolitionist, preacher, Underground Railroad conductor, and champion of women's suffrage. Mott, short in stature, preached to the black troops standing on a barrel so that she could be seen and heard. The soldiers sometimes stopped their drills to salute Mott, who watched them from her porch. The camp took its name from William Penn, the English Quaker who founded Philadelphia.

Thomas Webster, the Philadelphia merchant who chaired the Supervisory Committee, unveiled his recruiting strategy in an open letter to the *Liberator* signed by all sixty committee members in July 1863. Prefaced by a brief statement of the importance of defeating the Rebels and a description of black troops' courage under fire at recent battles at Port Hudson and Milliken's Bend, Louisiana, Webster then asked whites to donate funds to his cause, noting that the two Massachusetts regiments each had cost $25,000 to raise and equip. He next asked whites to help with recruiting, urging them in the tradition of the Massachusetts regiments to go beyond Pennsylvania's borders and to find suitable black recruits in Ohio and New York, states that had yet to begin enlisting blacks. Webster also reminded African Americans of their forbearers' valiant service in the American Revolution and the War of 1812 and of the praise showered on their ancestors by George Washington and Andrew Jackson. Webster exhorted men of color to match the spirit and pluck shown recently by their long-enslaved southern brethren and underscored the long-standing inequalities between whites and blacks. He closed by challenging blacks to take advantage of the chance to overthrow slavery and assert their manhood, an opportunity, Webster proclaimed, that had "no parallel in history." He admonished blacks that if they were to "shrink from it now [they would] . . . justify the taunts and sneers of [their] enemies and oppressors. Take advantage of it . . . and a grateful country . . . cannot refuse the applause which is the due of valor contending for the right."[24]

By late September the Supervisory Committee had raised three regiments. Enthusiastic to don the Union blue, a group of recruits penned a resolution that answered Webster's challenge. It read, "That we, the colored people of Philadelphia, throwing aside the unpleasant memories of the past, looking only to the future, and asking merely the same guaranties, the same open field and fair play that are given to our white fellow countrymen, desire here and now to express our willingness and readiness to come forward to the defence of our imperilled country."[25] In July, a thousand black men, accompanied by a brass band with drum and fife, marched to the homes of prominent Philadelphia whites, including Mayor Alexander Henry, serenading them with songs of appreciation and thanking them for their support. In addition, Philadelphia's African Methodist Episcopal clergymen encouraged blacks to sign up. Gradually mainstream white citizens came around to support the policy of arming blacks. They realized that black soldiers at the front would spare the lives of some whites and that black recruits counted against their state's enlistment quotas would thereby reduce the number of white recruits that federal authorities would call up.

Others remained unconvinced, however. In August authorities unexpectedly and inexplicably canceled the scheduled parade of a USCT regiment from Camp William Penn through downtown Philadelphia. An editorial in the *Liberator* speculated that Mayor Henry called off the parade in response to anonymous letters from whites protesting such a display of armed blacks. In October the 6th USCT, the last of the three regiments formed at Camp William Penn, did march along the city's major avenues—Walnut, Pine, and Broad Streets—on their way to board a steamer for travel to the South. Fearing a riot, Stearns took precautions to outfit the regiment's officers with hidden pistols and its rank and file with unloaded rifles.

While Stearns and Thomas recruited African American troops in Philadelphia, Ohio's governor David Tod, under mounting pressure from Lincoln to supply more men from his state, finally took advantage of John Mercer Langston's offer to assist him, but not, as Langston hoped, to recruit a black regiment. Rather, Tod sought Langston's help in encouraging Ohio blacks to join the Massachusetts regiments, organized into companies of Ohioans, units that would count against Ohio's draft quota. This approach, Tod explained, would provide the government with black troops more quickly than if Ohio had to start from scratch recruiting and training men of color. Langston declined. Ohio did not receive credit for black Ohioans who served in Massachusetts regiments, and the Massachusetts regiments did not organize their companies by the recruits' states of origin.

Tod finally had no choice but to ask Stanton for permission to raise a black regiment whose numbers would contribute toward Ohio's draft quota. Stanton agreed but required Tod to wait until the Massachusetts regiments filled up before raising one. By November 1863 Ohio had finally recruited its first black regiment, the 127th Ohio Volunteer Infantry (later the 5th USCT). Tod presented the regiment's colors to former Governor William Dennison Jr., who, along with Langston, had helped recruit the soldiers. At the colors ceremony Tod revealed his own ambivalence toward the recruitment of black troops in his state, explaining, "There were many men, and Abolitionists among them, who never had the least expectation of seeing a large portion of the colored men of Ohio formed into an orderly, well-drilled, and in every respect an efficient regiment."[26]

Recruiting in a Crossfire of Passions

Feelings ran high both for and against slavery in the border states, and not surprisingly, the question of raising black soldiers there remained volatile, especially in Lincoln's native state of Kentucky. Aware of the sensitivities of Unionist slaveholders along the borderland, and determined to keep the border states from joining the Confederacy, in February 1863 Congress authorized the president to recruit black troops in the border states but only with the permission of the respective state governors. Congress also forbade the recruiting of slaves belonging to masters loyal to the Union.

Masters with pro-Confederate leanings, however, lacked such an exclusion, meaning that those who recruited slaves from them did so at their peril, as Lieutenant Eben White, 7th USCT, discovered firsthand in October 1863. Accompanied by two enlisted men on an expedition to recruit slaves, White encountered John H. Sothoron and his son, Webster, on their plantation in Benedict, Maryland. The Sothorons were known to be Confederate sympathizers, visiting Richmond frequently and entertaining Confederate officers at their home. Upon witnessing the federal recruiters asking the Sothorons' slaves if they wished to enlist in the USCT, John Sothoron called White "a damned nigger-stealing son of a bitch" while Webster waved a revolver in his face and spat in the lieutenant's face. The older Sothoron told White not to interfere with his slaves, saying "you can't get 'em." White insisted that regardless of the Sothorons' protests he would take those slaves who wanted to enlist in the federal army. Then father and son each fired a single shot, killing White. As the black enlisted men ran for cover, one turned to see Webster smashing Lieutenant White's skull with the butt of his gun. The Sothorons abandoned their plantation and fled to the interior of the country.[27]

As the war dragged on, the need for Union manpower intensified so much that in 1864 Congress authorized the recruitment of slaves in the loyal border states regardless of their masters' loyalties. In April 1864 Stanton ordered the commander of the District of Kentucky, Brigadier General Stephen Gano Burbridge, a Kentucky slaveholder, to recruit black soldiers. In selecting Burbridge over Thomas and Stearns for the assignment, the secretary of war hoped to avoid stirring up the ire of Kentucky's Unionist slaveholders.

Thomas, either unaware of or unimpressed by Burbridge's appointment and the fragile politics of the situation, established his usual recruiting network of agents throughout the state. His move angered many.

Farmers petitioned Kentucky governor Thomas E. Bramlette, saying that Thomas's agents deprived them of all but helpless slaves. One of the petitioners, S. P. Cope, complained that Thomas's recruiters entered his house uninvited at breakfast searching for his "only remaining family Servant." The recruiters, Cope continued, caused "my grounds [to be] laid waste, my produce and stock despoiled and killed."[28] Stanton immediately informed Thomas that Burbridge was in charge of recruiting in Kentucky and ordered him to aid Burbridge in any way possible. The adjutant general sent Burbridge a roster of officers Thomas considered qualified to command Kentucky's newly forming black regiments and departed for the lower Mississippi valley.

In October 1864 Congress gave Burbridge's efforts a welcome boost when it authorized payment of $300 per slave recruited from any loyal slaveholder in the border states. No payment would be made for slaves whose owners supported the Rebels. Regardless of the owner's loyalties, Stanton decreed that all slaves recruited into the army would be free at the end of their service. As in other states, all black recruits counted against Kentucky's federal draft quota, thereby lessening the number of whites who would face the draft. Lincoln's government hoped that this would soften whites' opposition to transforming slaves into soldiers. The *Lowell (MA) Daily Citizen and News* commented favorably on Burbridge's success in recruiting blacks, commenting that whites would welcome the lower draft odds and that "the insane prejudices against colored men being allowed to fight against the rebels, has well nigh disappeared in all the Border states."[29]

Governor Bramlette no doubt disagreed with both the characterization of the border states' opposition to black soldiers as "insane prejudice" and with the assertion that opposition to that policy had disappeared. In a September 1864 letter to Lincoln, one of several that he sent protesting the recruitment of blacks in Kentucky, the governor explained defiantly, "We are preserving the right and liberties of our own race, and . . . are not willing to sacrifice a single life, or imperil the smallest right of free white men for the sake of the negro."[30] Though the president kept a close eye on black recruitment in Kentucky, neither it nor any of the other border states seceded, putting to rest one of Lincoln's biggest and most persistent fears. Burbridge, whom many of his fellow Kentuckians dubbed "Butcher Burbridge" for his harsh treatment of southern sympathizers, mustered in more than twenty thousand black soldiers by Christmas 1864. More soon followed.

Tennessee, a Confederate state largely under federal control and with a sizable Unionist population, presented an unusual situation for recruiting black troops. Conflicts between Washington, state and local officials, and a government-appointed recruiter, fed by deep divisions over slavery, complicated the black recruitment process in the Volunteer State. Once the Union army captured Nashville in February 1862, Lincoln commissioned Andrew Johnson Tennessee's military governor. He was a native of Unionist East Tennessee, a former slaveholder, and the only senator from a Confederate state to keep his seat in the U.S. Senate. In the summer of 1863 Stanton ordered Stearns to report to Nashville to begin recruiting black troops under Johnson's tacit supervision.

Johnson had been procuring slaves as laborers for a year prior to Stearns's arrival. Some had escaped from their masters to cross federal lines. Others arrived in Union army camps because their Unionist masters had voluntarily abandoned them. Still others had been hunted down on the streets of Nashville and impressed into the service by Yankee troops. Johnson put them all to work on Union railroads and fortifications and in hospitals for a promised wage of ten dollars a month—pay that they rarely received. Johnson's aggressive recruitment of slaves as military laborers left many of their families destitute. The men suffered from eighteen-hour days in extreme heat, poor food, and exposure at night from sleeping on hillsides without shelter.

Shortly before Stearns arrived in August 1863, federal recruiters impressed many able-bodied blacks into the 1st Alabama Infantry of African Descent (renamed the 55th USCT). Johnson, who resented Stearns's appointment and his commitment to the idea of black equality, worried that the out-of-state recruiter would interfere with his own recruitment efforts. Johnson wired Stanton, "We hope . . . that the organization of negro regiments in Tennessee will be left to the general commanding this department."[31] Stanton in turn wired Stearns, "All dissension is to be avoided, and if there is any want of harmony between you you had better leave Nashville and proceed to Cairo to await orders."[32] Learning of Johnson's priorities from Stanton, Lincoln wired the Tennessee military governor, explaining that recruiting soldiers should take precedence over recruiting laborers. Johnson took his cue from Lincoln and, secure in the knowledge that Stanton would back him in any disagreement with Stearns, let Stearns proceed in enlisting black Tennesseans.

Johnson, in the meantime, continued his practice of recruiting black laborers to complete the extension of the Nashville and Northwestern Railroad from Kingston Springs, Tennessee, westward to Johnsonville on the Tennessee River. Johnson's recruitment tactics—impressing blacks, even snatching them from church services and destroying passes of freedmen designed to exempt them from such impressments—horrified Stearns. Realizing, however, that he had no power to stop the impressments, Stearns commenced his usual recruiting practices. With the help of Captain Reuben D. Mussey Jr., a regular army officer with deep abolitionist convictions and later colonel of the 100th USCT, Stearns placed advertisements in newspapers, gave speeches, established recruiting stations, and sent the first companies of his blacks formed on scouting expeditions in and around Tennessee's capital.

Stearns sought to put the local citizenry at ease, assuring white Tennesseans that the recruitment of black troops posed threats to neither people nor property. While recruiting in Tennessee Stearns continued his mode of recruitment: caring for recruits' families by building camps to shelter and feed them, helping women find paying jobs as servants, establishing schools for girls, and instructing regimental chaplains to teach reading and writing. After three months in Nashville, Stearns had raised six regiments of USCT.

Beginning in February 1864 James T. Ayers, a white Kentuckian, itinerant Methodist preacher, and antislavery spokesman, began recruiting black soldiers for Mussey in the Tennessee valley. A zealous and successful recruiter, Ayers scoured the countryside in search of former slaves, determined to convince them to join Lincoln's army.

Most of the black troops Ayers recruited in northern Alabama served in the 17th USCT. Despite at times bungling his attempts to convince blacks to join the army, Ayers was reasonably successful, especially when he had armed black soldiers in tow to assist him. Historian John Hope Franklin explained Ayers's recruiting method:

After a town had been taken by the Union forces, Ayers would move in and proceed to enlist Negro recruits. He would nail up attractive posters provided by the Adjutant General's office and then would announce a meeting at which he would speak. If he succeeded in assembling a number of Negroes, he would appeal to them along two lines. In the first place, he would impress on his hearers the importance of getting into the fight in order to extend the blessings of liberty to their more unfortunate brothers who were still enslaved. Then, he would tell them that the ten dollars per month, food, and clothing would give them some semblance of security and independence.

Ayers insisted that in rural areas of the Tennessee valley he frequently was the first to inform slaves in Confederate-held territory of their freedom under the Emancipation Proclamation. This occurred, for example, as late as May 1864, at the Eldridge plantation near Huntsville, Alabama.[33]

Ayers complained frequently that recruiting men for the USCT was difficult work. He commonly encountered the ire of whites who branded him a troublemaker for whites and blacks alike. In one instance Ayers engaged in a heated exchange with the daughter of an Alabama planter who insulted him and said, "I want you always to know sir I hait you in my verry Hart." To this Ayers replied, "Your are A disgrace to the sects [sex]. Shame on you Siss." The recruiter then signed up four of her slaves as recruits for the 15th Tennessee Colored Regiment.[34]

Ayers found the initial reluctance and lack of enthusiasm by the slaves and ex-slaves to join the USCT surprising. He complained frequently that the blacks proffered all manner of excuses not to enlist. And though a zealous recruiter in what he considered a holy war against slavery, Ayers gradually became disappointed and disillusioned by the slow recruiting process. In September 1864 Ayers remarked that he was "hartily sick of Coaxing niggers to be Soaldiers Any more. They are so trifleing and mean the[y] dont Deserve to be free." Having said this, Ayers still believed that "perhaps I have in this way [as a recruiter of blacks troops] been of more service to my Country than in Any other way I could have been imployed, so all write." Yet despite his impatience with the slaves he encountered, Ayers never lost faith in the importance of their emancipation. "Those that have got out from under master are," he observed, "according to there Chance, making good crops of Corn and Cotton and seem to be striving to do as best they can." But eventually the rigors of recruiting wore him down. On September 13 Ayers resolved that "I am so tired of nigger Recruiting I am going as soon as A train goes through to Nashville to Resign and Go back to my Reg. or try."[35]

While on recruiting missions for Stearns, Colonel Thomas J. Morgan, commander of the 14th USCT, found black troops themselves to be his most potent recruiting tool. The sound of music, unfurled flags snapping in the breeze, and the sight of armed black men in new uniforms marching in precision excited many who saw them. Following a brief drill in a bare plantation yard or town square, the soldiers stood at ease. During one recruiting event in Nashville, Jerry Sullivan, an ex-slave turned USCT sergeant, stepped forward and called to a crowd of black folk in the manner of a Baptist preacher: "God is in this war. He will lead us on to victory. . . . Come, boys, let's get some guns from Uncle Sam, and go coon hunting; shooting those gray back coons that go poking about the country now a days. . . . Don't ask your wife, for if she is a wife worth having she will call you a coward for asking her. . . . I've got a wife and she says to me, the other day, 'Jerry, if you don't go to the war mighty soon, I'll go off and leave you, as some of the Northern gentlemen want me to go home to cook for them.' "[36]

When recruiting blacks for the 1st Arkansas Volunteer Infantry Regiment of African Descent (later the 46th USCT) in Helena, Arkansas, Captain Lindley Hoffman Miller, a New Jersey officer with antislavery convictions, used the "Marching Song of the First Arkansas (Negro) Regiment" to instill potential enlistees to sign up. Miller wrote the song, a parody set to the tune of "John Brown's Body," to underscore black pride, militancy, and the drive for full equality. The song ended with the lyrics:

> Den fall'in, colored bredren, you'd better do it soon,
> Don't you hear de drum a –beatin' de Yankee Doodle tune?
> We are wid you now dis mornin', we'll be far away by noon,
> As we go marching on.[37]

Northern recruiters for the USCT often encountered much the same resistance and prejudice from whites as that experienced by recruiting agents in the border states and Confederate South. New York City proved to be a tragic case in point. The state's governor, Horatio Seymour, a Democrat and vocal critic of Lincoln, refused to authorize black regiments. Following the final Emancipation Proclamation, Seymour continued his opposition to recruiting blacks, which, in hindsight, may have been of little consequence, as the prejudices and fears of many in New York City probably would have impeded recruitment attempts anyway. In July 1863 those prejudices and fears turned ugly.

On July 8 New York City police superintendent John A. Kennedy telegrammed Stanton asking him to cancel plans for the 55th Massachusetts Volunteers to embark for the South from the city's port. "Every day," Kennedy wrote, "my men are engaged in protecting negroes from—unjustifiable attacks. . . . Save us from riot and possible bloodshed by letting these Massachusetts troops be transported from a sea-port nearer their encampment than this is."[38] Stanton then telegrammed Governor Andrew, informing him that "events on the Mississippi may render a change of destination for your colored regiments very desirable. You will therefore retain them in Boston until further orders."[39]

Kennedy saw his worst fears realized on July 11 when Irish and German laborers took to the streets in a three-day rampage, the infamous New York City Draft Riots. Several factors brought on the racial disturbance. For six months conservative journalists and Democratic politicians had predicted that Lincoln's emancipation edict would result in blacks flooding into the city to take the jobs of working-class whites. A federal draft law subjected all married white male citizens, except those exempted by virtue of holding a military-related job such as telegraph operator, between ages 20 and 35 and all single white male citizens between ages 35 and 45 to a draft lottery. Those who could pay the government a $300 commutation fee or hire a substitute could avoid military service. The draft, to the anger of whites, did not apply to blacks, for they were not yet citizens. The July 11 drawing of the draft lottery sparked the riots.

In twenty minutes the rioters, none of whom could afford the $300 fee or had the funds to hire a substitute, laid waste to the four-story Colored Orphans Society on Fifth Avenue. Fortunately the school's superintendent managed to escort all 233 children out the back door as the mob broke down the front door. White longshoremen destroyed businesses and residences along the docks—brothels, dance halls, boardinghouses, and tenements— that catered to blacks. Rioters lynched blacks from lampposts, cutting one black man's dead body down and dragging the corpse through the streets. In one instance whites stoned a black sailor to death in front of a crowd of spectators. Landlords drove blacks from their residences in order to avoid the mob's wrath. By week's end, eleven blacks had been hanged, hundreds of black families had fled the city for New Jersey, and businesses lay in ruin. Draft riots also occurred in other places, including Newark, New Jersey, and Albany, New York, as well as rural counties in Indiana and Illinois.

The riots and Seymour's obstructionism delayed but did not prevent New York City from supplying black regiments to the Union army. In November, when passions had subsided, a group of prominent New Yorkers, including William Cullen Bryant, editor of the *New York Evening Post*, and Brigadier

General John Cochrane, Major General Daniel E. Sickles, along with businessman William E. Dodge and others formed the New York Association for Colored Volunteers. The group successfully petitioned Stanton for permission to raise black regiments under national, not state, auspices, thereby trumping Seymour's opposition to the project. Black New Yorkers rushed to the colors from throughout the state to form the 20th USCT. Significantly, they garnered a $300 bounty, the same bounty white enlistees received. Another recruiting committee, made up of members of the Union League Club, paid ten dollars to anyone who brought a black recruit in good health to one of the recruiting centers. The 20th USCT mustered into service on Rikers Island in the East River in February 1864. A month later, en route south on a steamer, in what the *New York Times* called "infallible tokens of a new epoch," the regiment marched "down our gayest avenues and our busiest thoroughfares with waving handkerchiefs, flowers, acclamation."[40] The Union League Club presented the men with a parchment scroll signed by some of New York City's wealthiest men and, symbolically, one woman, Mrs. Robert Gould Shaw.

In spite of many obstacles—the animosity directed toward them by whites, unequal pay, excess fatigue duty, worries about families left behind, and impressments—African Americans continued to muster into federal forces until they made up roughly 10 percent of the soldiers who fought for the Union.

3 How White Officers Learned to Command Black Troops

ONCE STEARNS began recruiting black troops, Stanton and Lincoln turned their attention to the question of who would lead them. Both knew public opinion would not tolerate blacks as commissioned officers. A white soldier complained to a *New York Herald* reporter that if he found himself reporting to a black officer, "I must not only obey him, but I must politely touch my cap when I approach him. I must stand while he sits, unless his Captainship should condescendingly ask me to be seated. Negro soldiers are all very well," he continued, "but let us have white officers, whom we can receive and treat as equals everywhere, and whom we may treat as superiors without humiliation."[1]

In January 1863 a clash between white and black troops on Ship Island, a barrier island twelve miles off the coast of Mississippi, showed just what could happen if whites served under blacks. The situation resulted when General Nathaniel P. Banks sent seven companies of the 2nd Louisiana Native Guards to join two companies of the all-white 13th Maine Volunteer Regiment, who had been holding the island. Banks ordered the Maine troops' commander to turn over command of his forces to Colonel Nathan W. Daniels of the 2nd Louisiana Native Guards, all of whose officers, in a rare exception to the white-officers-only rule, were black. Daniels ordered the nine companies to consolidate in a way that required equal treatment of soldiers of both races.

The move put black captains in the Native Guards over white lieutenants in the Maine unit. The Maine soldiers refused to obey Daniels's consolidation order. Daniels arrested the white troops, took their guns and equipment, stationed armed black soldiers around their quarters, and ordered them to surrender as prisoners. To avoid violence, the whites acceded to Daniels's order. Banks, eager to quell the incident, quickly removed the Maine companies from Ship Island. "White and black troops should not be brigaded together or stationed together," read an editorial about the event in the *New York Times*, which proclaimed, "At all events, there must be on no account be occasion furnished for collisions between our white and black soldiers in that Department."[2] Any thoughts of commissioning blacks as officers perished after the Ship Island incident. Stanton had to move quickly to establish a process of recruiting, training, and putting into the field thousands of white commissioned officers to lead the ever-growing number of black troops.

Obtaining Commissions

Whites obtained commissions in several ways. State governors appointed officers, an approach Governor Andrew had taken with Robert Gould Shaw. Some whites became officers as a reward for raising a regiment of black soldiers. Still other whites, looking for more promising opportunities, as well as higher pay and status, left their white regiments to gain a higher rank in a black regiment. Most of those who sought to advance in rank in a USCT regiment first had to pass muster before one of the various boards established to vet officer candidates. A few prepared for their board examination by attending the nation's first officer candidate school, Philadelphia's Free Military School for Applicants for Commands of Colored Troops, established on December 26, 1863.[3] Those charged with recruiting and selecting officer candidates typically identified men who combined high moral standards with military experience and abolitionist views.

Governor Andrew, for instance, looked for white "young men of military experience, of firm anti-slavery principles, ambitious, superior to a vulgar contempt for color, and having faith in the capacity of colored men for military service."[4] Andrew explained to Francis Shaw, Robert Gould Shaw's father, that he had used these criteria in choosing his son to command the 54th Massachusetts Volunteers.

Lorenzo Thomas took a similar tack in selecting white commissioned officers for the black troops he recruited in the Mississippi valley. Faced in 1863 with raising twenty regiments, each requiring thirty-five commissioned officers, Thomas immediately had seven hundred commissions to fill. He looked first to the white volunteer units, offering privates, corporals, and sergeants the appealing prospect of promotion to sergeant, lieutenant, captain, major, or even colonel while, at the same time, dampening whites' fears about the use of black soldiers. Whites would lead them. Thomas made clear, however, that in his search for officers, he "desire[d] none but those well qualified and whose heart is in the work."[5] When Thomas learned of a lieutenant colonel in an Ohio regiment whose anti-black prejudice prevented his "heart from being in it," the adjutant general cashiered the officer from the service. At a New Year's Day party in Nashville, Tennessee, the officer had refused to shake the hand of Colonel Thomas J. Morgan of the 14th USCT.

Each USCT regiment also required a cadre of noncommissioned officers: a sergeant major, a quartermaster sergeant, ten company first sergeants, twenty sergeants, and forty corporals. Thomas at first filled such positions with whites. He soon discontinued that practice after concluding that most white appointees were insufficiently antislavery in their convictions and that many accepted their stripes only because they represented a promotion, higher pay, and increased authority. Thomas then asked a black regiment's white colonel to choose noncommissioned officers from among the regiment's black troops. Colonels soon found that most former slaves' inability to read or write limited that pool of possible noncommissioned officers. Thomas next turned to the more literate free black population from the northern and western states as a source of noncommissioned officers. He also encouraged chaplains, officers' wives, and interested white soldiers to teach the men of the USCT to read and write.

Many whites who applied for officer positions did so because their hearts were truly in it. In his letter to Andrew applying for an officer's position, J. W. M. Appleton wrote:

> I am desirous of serving our Country in connection with the colored troops now being raised. . . . I am induced . . . by the belief that the two great problems that demand our attention in connection with the freedom of the slave are Firstly, Will the freed-man work for his living—Secondly will he fight for his liberty? I believe that he will do both and I desire to assist him to do the latter.[6]

Another soldier sought a commission with a USCT unit because he wanted military action. Writing to his parents, Sergeant Henry Crydenwise remarked, "Now is the time to prove that I am what I have always professed to be—an Abolitionist."[7] He was motivated to leave his white unit for a black one after his superiors had ignored evidence that Crydenwise had gathered proving that a white soldier had killed a black man. "A negroes life is little more regarded than that of a dog," the sergeant complained. "Tis time something was done," he continued, "to teach people a negroes life cannot be taken with impunity for every slight offence."[8]

Yet other soldiers applied for commissions in black units determined to receive the higher pay, better rations, and prestige that accompanied promotion as an officer in the USCT. Thomas sometimes failed to detect such motives. "I would drill a company of aligators for a hundred and twenty a month," an Illinois soldier confided to a friend.[9] "You know that, with my restless disposition, I could not be contented as a brigade bugler while there was a possibility of doing better," a Pennsylvania soldier informed his sister.[10] Some determined to retire as an officer whenever they pleased, an option in black units unavailable in white ones. Except under unusual circumstances Stanton refused such requests starting in 1864. Others hoped that their experience with the USCT would become a ticket to West Point and thereby to obtaining a commission in the regular army after the war.

Dissatisfaction with a unit or commanding officer prompted a number of applications for commissions. For example, Marshall Harvey Twitchell, a sergeant with the 4th Vermont Volunteer Regiment applied for and won a captaincy after his commander twice had passed him over for promotion. Others, like Major General Robert H. Milroy, an Indiana native and graduate of Norwich Academy, applied to lead the USCT out of a quest for redemption. In June 1862 Milroy had disobeyed orders to withdraw his troops during the Second Battle of Winchester (Virginia). His action resulted in the capture of thirty-four hundred Union soldiers and loss of numerous artillery pieces and supply wagons. His court-martial panel relieved him of command and assigned him to work as a recruiter under Major General George Henry Thomas. Milroy asked Stanton for permission to "recruit and organize" a black regiment, noting that "though kept out of the ring of active service for near two years I am not unworthy of my present rank."[11] Stanton disagreed and denied Milroy's request.

Foreigners, who stood little chance of obtaining commissions in the regular army, found commissions in black regiments within their reach. Edelmiro Mayer, a member of the Argentinean Army who had fought in thirty-two battles over the course of ten years before immigrating to the United States, obtained a captaincy in the 4th USCT in 1863. He left the service two years later as a lieutenant colonel. At least 265 of the 7,100 officers of the USCT were immigrants from German-speaking countries. The majority migrated from Prussia and the other German states that Bismarck later cobbled together into a unified Germany. Others came from the Austro-Hungarian Empire, Switzerland, and Denmark. They were a diverse lot—abolitionists, adventurers, careerists, philanthropists, and racists. Most already had served in the volunteer ranks and considered a commission in the segregated USCT an improvement over their enlisted service with white troops. As officers they received higher status, better pay, and improved accommodations, and stood a greater chance of survival than did enlisted men. Whatever their motivations for joining the USCT, German American officers were among the first whites to join African American fighting units. By war's end German American officers participated in almost every major battle the USCT fought, from Milliken's Bend (June 7, 1863) to New Market Heights (September 30, 1864). Forty-three served as field and staff officers. Four—Colonels Ignatz Kappner, Hermann Lieb, Ladislas Zsulavszki, and Carl Bentzoni—commanded USCT regiments. Eighteen German-speaking immigrants served as assistant or regimental surgeons. Fifteen held the rank of lieutenant colonel, and six received commissions as major.

Officer Recruiting Processes

The growing need for officers soon outstripped the capacity of governors and generals to identify enough capable officers to lead the burgeoning number of black troops. Lincoln's government clearly needed a comprehensive and systematic process of identifying USCT officers. In May 1863 the Bureau of Colored Troops stepped in to meet that need by coordinating recruiting officers in the North. General Lorenzo Thomas established a process to do the same in the Mississippi valley and the West. Applicants wrote letters to Thomas or Major Charles W. Foster accompanied by recommendations. Most explained why they wanted to officer black troops. Often the applicant's commanding officer composed the letter and circulated it among other officers to add their endorsements. Typical recommendations described the aspiring officer's combat experiences and assured the recipient that the soldier in question possessed the highest moral values. In order to be considered for an appointment as an officer in the USCT, civilian candidates required letters from prominent citizens praising their character.

An officer in a white unit occasionally obstructed the system by refusing to recommend a soldier he did not want to lose or magnifying one's qualifications while failing to mention defects, including fondness for liquor or gambling. In some cases undetected defects in an officer candidate led to a newly appointed officer being forced to resign his commission.

Thomas and Foster selected those applicants who appeared promising on paper to appear before an oral examining board consisting of three to five officers. They examined candidates at one of the major examination centers established in Washington, DC, New Orleans, Nashville, Cincinnati, Saint Louis, and Davenport, Iowa, or before divisional boards such as the ones Thomas established in Stevenson, Alabama, and Chattanooga, Tennessee. To succeed at the oral examination, the applicant needed to demonstrate an appropriate level of knowledge depending on the rank he sought. Because the War Department had not yet established specific requirements, Thomas established them for the USCT. Lieutenants needed to be able to read and write, be conversant with grammar, and be thoroughly versed in company movements. In order to be appointed captain (who would command a company), the applicant would be responsible for describing the operations of a battalion.

Members of the various boards had basically the same expectations, questioning applicants to determine their knowledge of tactics, army regulations, military knowledge, mathematics, history, and geography. Colonel Reuben D. Mussey, who chaired the Nashville board, gave specific instructions to his examiners on how they should conduct the examinations: "Do not ask leading questions; do not seek to refresh the candidate's memory; do not inform him whether his answer is correct; you are to examine, not teach him."[12] General Thomas exempted quartermaster candidates, who would be dispersing supplies to the troops, from questions about tactics. They were, however, responsible for demonstrating knowledge of War Department regulations as well as the methods and systems of accounting for and distributing supplies and provisions.

An examination could consist of up to several hundred questions depending on the military rank the candidate sought. Major J. Smith Brown, an applicant for a colonelcy, answered 293 questions before the Saint Louis board over the course of two and a half to three hours. Horace Bumstead, who received a major's commission, answered forty-nine questions on tactics plus follow-up questions. Typical questions on tactics included the number of ranks that formed a company, the distance between the ranks, and the position of the lieutenant colonel and the major when in column. Other questions included the distance between battalions in column at half distance and the general's role before closing the column of a subdivision in rear of a battery. The examiners often began with questions related to military matters and ended with general knowledge questions, such as identifying the largest city in the United States, distinguished men of ancient times, and the greatest generals of modern times. The boards questioned the candidate about his knowledge of Greek, Latin, algebra, geometry, and physics. Examiners scored an applicant's performance on a scale of one to nine, one to seven, or one to five. The highest number usually denoted the top score.

More than nine thousand men applied for USCT commissions. Of that number the BCT approved nearly four thousand examinees. Approximately one in four of the applicants received a commission. Enlisted men who failed the examination either completed their term of enlistment with their white unit or returned to private life. The War Department discharged from the service officers who left their white unit to take the examination to serve with a USCT unit and failed.

The USCT officer selection process was more rigorous than that used in the white volunteer regiments—election by one's peers or appointment by a state governor. The procedure implemented by the BCT to identify officers generally produced a higher caliber of leaders than those who commanded white units. "It is clear that the selective system for officering those forces did produce leaders substantially better qualified than those who led the white volunteer army in the first two years of the war," concluded historian Dudley Taylor Cornish.[13]

The case of Ohioan Samuel Evans suggests the motives of some who sought reassignment to and promotion with the USCT. Evans, a private in the 70th Ohio Volunteer Infantry, left that unit to become a lieutenant in the 59th USCT. He justified the move to his father, who doubted its wisdom. "My place is easier than a privates," Evans explained. "[I] have better quarters and more privileges." He also maintained "that a Negro is no better than a white man and has just as good a right to fight for his freedom and the government."[14]

Another USCT officer, Major John McMurray of the 6th USCT, left no explanation of why he decided to serve with a black regiment. A private in the 57th Pennsylvania Volunteer Regiment, he learned of the organization of African American regiments and quickly secured the necessary recommendations and invitation to Washington to appear before an examination board headed by Major General Silas Casey, a West Point graduate and nationally recognized authority on infantry tactics and the training of recruits. After waiting for ten days, McMurray received his call to be examined. Later he recalled that "nearly all the questions being asked me [were] by General Casey in person," and added,

> I was very nervous throughout this examination, and felt that I had acquitted myself poorly. I remember distinctly one question the General asked me. It was this: "If you were commanding a regiment, and it was marching in line of battle, if you wanted it to form a hollow square, what command would you give, and how would the movement be executed?" It so happened that in reading the tactics over and over, my attention had been specially directed to that movement. I had it thoroughly fixed in my mind, and was able to give the proper command, and to describe in detail, with precision, all the minutia of the movement. My answer, given promptly, and without hesitation, seemed to please the General greatly, as I was informed afterward that that was a favorite tactical movement of his.

Forty hours after his interview an orderly from the Adjutant General's Office brought McMurray the news he craved. He had been appointed a captain in the 6th USCT and was ordered to report to the regiment at Camp William Penn.[15]

Notwithstanding the rigor of the BCT's selection process, it did not guarantee a complaint-free process. A major of engineers in the USCT who failed to gain promotion to lieutenant colonel groused that the test failed to address the subject of engineering seriously. "The questions asked were oral, no problems given to solve, no propositions to demonstrate, no written examples required," lamented the disgruntled officer. "The examination," he concluded, "was a farce."[16] Even those who passed their test registered complaints. Daniel Densmore, who passed his examination for major, told his brother, "Boots properly blacked would rate as high as a problem well solved."[17]

As in all armies, many promotions in the USCT became mired in red tape. And not surprisingly, those whose applications languished queried Thomas. Albert Lloyd, chief clerk in the Saint Louis Judge Advocate's Office, wrote, "As I have understood that other applications of a more recent date have been replied to, I thought it probable mine may have miscarried."[18] Others, such as Clarence Laird of Covington, Kentucky, passed the officer examination but never received a commission (he had applied for a captaincy). Laird alerted Thomas to his predicament and expressed his determination to join a black regiment. Hearing nothing after several months, Laird returned home, complaining to Thomas that "it would have been an act of justice to grant my request."[19]

Other selection irregularities included the rare occurrence of the New Orleans board recommending Captain Edward Martindale for a colonelcy even though he had failed the required examination. Politicians sometimes obtained commissions for favored individuals without the candidate having even bothered to take the examination. Senator Henry Wilson of Massachusetts, the powerful chairman of the Senate Military Affairs Committee, procured a second lieutenancy in the USCT for Albert Austin in this manner. Stanton gave Tennessee military governor Andrew Johnson the authority to appoint all commissioned officers for units raised in Tennessee, thereby exempting them from the examination process.

Despite these irregularities, the selection process for USCT officers generally prevented the appointment of a categorically unqualified officer. In the case of Ohio's first black unit, the 127th Ohio Volunteer Infantry (soon redesignated the 5th USCT), Governor Tod wanted Captain Lewis McCoy to command the regiment. Captain McCoy, however, qualified for a captaincy, which he refused to accept, but not a colonelcy. McCoy continued, nevertheless, to command the 127th Ohio during its formation and training at Camp Delaware, near Columbus. The troops liked McCoy and preferred him over the regiment's eventual commander, Colonel James W. Conine, who had passed the examination for colonel. As the regiment departed Camp Delaware for Virginia in November 1863, the troops gave McCoy, who stayed behind, a gold watch chain and his wife a gold ring. Had the 5th USCT been a white regiment, Tod's preference and the troops' sentiments would have prevailed, and McCoy would have led the regiment.

Completion of the selection and examination processes signaled that a soldier possessed the knowledge and character required of a USCT officer. But it gave no indication of crucial intangible qualities, including the ability to make the right decisions quickly under stressful conditions. Colonel George W. Baird was one whose combat achievements squared poorly with his examination performance. As a private in the War Department's Invalid Corps, Baird reportedly received the highest score ever given by the Washington, DC, examination board and possessed impeccable recommendations for his commission. But he struggled with command responsibilities with the 32nd USCT once in the field. Baird participated in the doomed Union effort at the Battle of Honey Hill on November 30, 1864.

Corporal Robert K. Beecham of the 2nd Wisconsin Volunteers took a circuitous path to his commission with the USCT. He served in the famous Iron Brigade (a nickname bestowed on the unit by Major General George B. McClellan for the Brigade's uncommon bravery in combat) from May 1861 until his capture by the Confederates at Gettysburg in July 1863. Following his exchange through the prisoner-of-war cartel, Beecham stood for examination for an officer's commission in the USCT. Committed to black uplift yet unimpressed by what he described disparagingly as "the fraternity of military swell heads"—the officer corps—Beecham passed his exam and received a commission as lieutenant in the 23rd USCT. He described tongue-in-cheek the entire examination experience whereby he joined the ranks of "the mighty, with the magnificent privilege of snubbing a private soldier as much as I wanted to, and indulging in the senseless show of official 'fuss and feathers.'" More seriously, Beecham believed that the examination system was democratic and attractive for "ambitious young men" such as himself. He considered the process "delightfully easy . . . for a private soldier who possesses the physical manhood, the intellectual ability and the sand in his craw to get a commission in the American army."[20]

Beecham obviously possessed those qualities. In the winter 1863–64 he drilled black recruits, mostly men from Baltimore and Washington, D.C. His wife came east and helped open a school for the men of the 23rd. After guarding supply lines during the first half of 1864, Beecham and his black troops fought at the bloody Battle of the Crater in July 1864, where he was wounded and once again incarcerated by the Confederates. After eight months in prison Beecham escaped.

A School for Officers

General Casey, with Stanton's backing, led the federal government's efforts to establish and maintain high standards for the selection and appointment of USCT officers. Casey mandated that successful applicants for commissions be physically fit, morally sound, literate, and knowledgeable about geography, history, and military tactics.

By September 1863 Casey had developed the Washington board to the point where many considered it the army's most rigorous, with only 53 percent of those appearing before what contemporaries dubbed the "Casey Board" passing. Most applicants who failed possessed admirable combat backgrounds but lacked, as Casey explained to Philadelphia's Thomas Webster, "a few weeks close study of the principles of tactics and the details of army regulations."[21]

For his part, Webster had been struggling to find competent officers to train the black troops that had answered his recruiting calls. Encouraged by Casey's letter, in December 1863 Webster established the Free Military School for Applicants for Commands of Colored Troops. Webster considered his school's purpose "to take hold of men who are prompted by the right motives to seek command of colored troops and reveal to them their deficiencies, assist them in overcoming them—and prepare them for examination."[22] Reflecting the prevailing view of the day among liberal whites, Webster believed that prejudice and slavery had so destroyed the black man's dignity, self-reliance, and individuality that only white men with strong intellects and solid morals could lead them. Placing the black soldier in the hands of lesser officers, Webster feared, would awaken blacks' alleged barbarous temperament on the battlefield, thereby exacerbating whites' fears of black savagery and cruelty. This in turn would block any chance for African Americans to become citizens.

Prospective students underwent a physical examination upon arrival at Webster's school. Colonel John J. Taggart, the chief preceptor, interviewed them and placed each of the new officer candidates in one of three classes: the School of the Soldier and Company (for the novice students), the School of the Battalion (for the most advanced students), or the School of the Company, depending on the students' knowledge. Students could be promoted during their course of study on an instructor's recommendation. Unusually gifted students could avoid instruction altogether and proceed directly to Washington to take Casey's examination if they passed a special test. The typical student at the Free Military School was a man in his early twenties who came from Pennsylvania. He possessed a common school education and had labored as a farmer or clerk prior to enrolling in a volunteer regiment as a private or noncommissioned officer. Students paid no tuition but were responsible for their room and board.

Webster modeled the curriculum on the examinations administered by Washington's "Casey Board." Students used Casey's own three-volume *Infantry Tactics, for the Instruction, Exercise, and Manoeuvres of the Soldier, a Company, Line of Skirmishers, Battalion, Brigade, or Corps d'Armée* (1862). They spent a month to six weeks at the school and received three hours of classroom instruction every day but Sunday. Instructors filled the rest of the students' six days per week with drill, drill parade, and evening study. Strict discipline prevailed. Students could be dismissed or punished for failing to give undivided attention to teachers, defacing books, disrupting class with loud talk, forging attendance rolls, skipping drill, being absent without leave for more than three days, or smoking. Instructors could bring students before Taggart for disciplinary purposes. Between graduation and appearing before Casey's examination board in Washington, students commuted to Camp William Penn, where they instructed and drilled black recruits under the supervision of experienced officers. This field practicum gave the USCT officers-to-be their only hands-on training.

When a student considered himself prepared to take the school's two-day exam, a professor tested him on the academic subjects the first day. On day two Taggart examined the student on military tactics. Those who passed went to Washington to face Casey.

Ninety-six percent of Webster's students passed the "Casey Board" examination, a decided improvement over the former success rate of 53 percent. Many passed with distinction, with 13 percent attaining the rank of major or higher in the USCT. Prior to the school's existence, only 3 percent earned a major's rank or above. Altogether, the Free Military School produced about five hundred commissioned officers (colonels, lieutenant colonels, majors, captains, and first and second lieutenants). This constituted a large cadre of officers to be sure, but only a fraction of the approximately seven thousand officers assigned to USCT regiments.

The Free Military School's teach-to-the-test curriculum remained unchanged throughout its short history except for one addition Webster initiated when, in January 1864, he hired a professor of ethical education. Reports of a mutiny sparked by officer brutality on December 9, 1863, at Fort Jackson, a Mississippi River garrison seventy miles below New Orleans, prompted the addition. Lieutenant Colonel Augustus C. Benedict of the 4th Corps d'Afrique Infantry (later the 76th USCT), routinely whipped troops, mostly former slaves. He reportedly struck his men with his fist and with his sword, tied soldiers up by their thumbs with their toes just reaching the ground, and ordered soldiers to "spread a man on his back, drive stakes down, and spread his hands and feet, take off his shoes, and take molasses and spread it on his face, hands, and feet." One soldier spent two days in this condition.[23]

The breaking point for the men of the 4th Corps d'Afrique came when Benedict horsewhipped two band members. Troops rushed to the parade ground yelling, "Kill the d——d Yankees." Many cried, "Give us Colonel Benedict. . . . Kill Colonel Benedict," and released prisoners from the regimental guardhouse.[24] A court-martial board, which took testimony from the white officers only, handed down sentences of one month to twenty years at hard labor to nine of the thirteen soldiers tried. A musician received a sentence of one year at hard labor. The board acquitted two soldiers and sentenced two others to execution by firing squad. (They avoided execution but were imprisoned in Fort Jefferson, Dry Tortugas, Florida.) As for Lieutenant Colonel Benedict, the board dismissed him from the service for "inflicting cruel and unusual punishment, to the prejudice of good order and military discipline." Benedict's case unfortunately did not end officer misconduct in the 4th Corps d'Afrique. In January 1864 four white officers were accused of rape or attempted rape of several of the black laundresses attached to the troubled regiment. Though Brigadier General William Dwight recommended their dishonorable discharge, President Lincoln revoked the officers' dismissals.[25]

The extent to which the added ethics course prevented graduates from abusing their power remains unknown, but the overall success of the Free Military School in preparing commissioned officers prompted Webster to initiate an auxiliary school in March 1864, where preceptors and advanced students tutored twenty-one blacks in the duties of a noncommissioned officer. The auxiliary school closed before any of its students could complete their studies. Financial problems forced the Free Military School to close on September 15, 1864. But it stands as the first officer candidate school in American military history.

Confronting the Rigors of Field Command

As thorough as their selection and training processes had been, once in the field, large challenges nonetheless confronted the new USCT officers. Not all who passed the board examinations, including Casey's, found field command easy or to their liking. Regardless of where or how a USCT officer received his assignment, his first task became forming new relationships. Accepting a commission meant leaving one's white regiment, which usually consisted of friends and relatives recruited with him from his neighborhood, town, or county. The white officer assigned to the USCT could end up leading a group of soldiers none of whom he knew individually or as a group. For many the new command represented the officer's first extended contact with men of color. In addition, as per the Confederate Congress's joint resolutions of April and May 1863 ordering the execution of Union officers for "inciting servile insurrection" and the reenslavement of captured black troops, all USCT officers knew that they faced possible execution if captured. Many thus experienced feelings of loneliness, isolation, and anxiety upon reporting to their black regiments.

Racist attitudes of officers, family, and friends frequently gave little comfort to the new USCT officer as he settled into his assignment. A New York artilleryman's decision to apply for a chaplaincy with the USCT elicited the wrath of his brother-in-law, who exclaimed, "A chaplain of a *nigger* regiment! My God! deliver him in due time from falling into that error."[26] In another instance, a father told his son who had expressed interest in serving in a USCT regiment, "I had much rath[er] you had not asked my opinion, or even informed me, that you were making yourself so willing, to accept a degraded position. I wouth [sic] rather clean out S——t houses at ten cents pr day, then [sic] to take you[r] position with its pay."[27] Such stern disapproval deterred neither soldier from joining the black troops. Nor did the possible social opprobrium from joining the USCT discourage Sergeant Henry Crydenwise from serving with African Americans. "With some," the New Yorker wrote, "I should loose [sic] caste by becoming an officer in a colored regiment but I cannot think that the petty prejudices or even the frown of others should deter us from persuing [sic] what we conceive to be a line of duty."[28] Other whites received support from friends and family for their decision to join the USCT. A father in Minnesota told his son that his appointment "is perhaps a thankless service but nevertheless important and if successful may aid in the cultivation of the blacks to a capacity they might not have attained in civil life among the 'chivalry' even were they emancipated by them and the utmost favor allowed possible in such society."[29]

Some officers of African American troops generated support for themselves by convincing comrades from their white units to join them. For example, forty-four soldiers from the 4th Illinois Calvary became officers in the 3rd U.S. Colored Cavalry. Eighteen men from the 128th New York Volunteer Regiment served together as officers in the 90th USCT.

Blacks Gain and Lose Commissions

Though whites held most officer positions in the USCT, a few blacks did attain the elusive status of commissioned officer. The largest group consisted of the more than seventy-five who served in the five regiments of Louisiana Native Guards (three of which Butler had federalized in 1862). To recruit the other two regiments, Butler solicited the help of a group of twenty free blacks who had been lieutenants and captains in the three Confederate militia regiments and who had remained as civilians in New Orleans following its fall. Butler asked the former officers to raise two regiments. One of them asked, "General, shall we be officers as we were before?" "Yes, every one of you who is fit to be an officer shall be, and all the line officers shall be colored men," Butler assured them.[30] Butler had his two regiments ten days later.

The African Americans did not hold their commissions for long, however. General Banks, who replaced Butler in December 1862, had other ideas about blacks serving as officers in the USCT. During the next eighteen months he established boards to examine the black officers for fitness. The panels consisted of junior white officers who stood to be promoted into the positions of black officers found unfit. Not surprisingly, Banks's examining board deemed many of the black officers unqualified, and the general accordingly replaced most of them with whites.

Banks intervened directly when he ordered a group of sixteen black officers to leave their post in Baton Rouge and report to him in New Orleans. When they arrived, Banks told the stunned officers that they had best resign their commissions, as the federal government did not recognize their rank. All sixteen resigned on the spot rather than face what they anticipated would be a humiliating dismissal. On their return to Baton Rouge the blacks found that their white replacements had already been appointed. Banks had kept their resignations a secret. The officers filed a protest with the War Department but to no avail.

Black troops, on the other hand, believed that their own people would make excellent officers. A corporal in the 54th Massachusetts, James Henry Gooding, noted that many sergeants in his regiment "were just as capable of being entrusted with the command of colored troops as those who know nothing of the disposition or feelings of such troops."[31]

Six blacks did manage to gain commissions in Massachusetts regiments thanks to Governor Andrew, who nominated Sergeants Steven A. Swails of the 54th Massachusetts and James M. Trotter of the 55th Massachusetts along with four other noncommissioned officers to the rank of second lieutenant in the spring of 1864. The War Department initially blocked the promotions by refusing to allow the men to muster out at their last rank (which all non-commissioned officers slated for promotion had to do before they could muster back in at their higher grade). But by early 1865, the army, in the face of continued success in the field by black troops and the growing support from high-level government officials, relented and commissioned the six men as second lieutenants. The promotions did not sit well with many of the white officers, but as Trotter explained, "All the best officers are in favor of it."[32]

One of those officers, J. W. M. Appleton, by then a major with the 54th Massachusetts, said of Andrew's appointments: "This is another step forward. And Old Massachusetts takes it. A colored man given a fairly won Commission. We are very proud of it."[33] In February 1865 the War Department issued its highest rank to date to an African American when it commissioned Martin R. Delany a major in the infantry, though he never held field command. A year earlier, six white military surgeons wrote President Lincoln, complaining that Dr. Alexander T. Augusta, a black surgeon commissioned a major, commanded them at Maryland's Camp Stanton. Despite Augusta's rank and seniority they refused to serve under him. Augusta was reassigned.[34]

4 How Blacks Became Soldiers

ONCE IN CAMP, officers and recruits alike confronted the realities of forming combat-ready regiments under trying circumstances. Officers, many of whom had previously met few if any blacks, assumed responsibility for leading them. Most of the men in their commands could neither read nor write and had little or no experience with weapons or military discipline. The men of the U.S. Colored Troops, like soldiers in all wars, lived relatively spartan lives. Their equipment, food, and living conditions often left much to be desired. Nevertheless, black troops served—and served well—under both separate and unequal conditions. They received unequal pay, performed a disproportionate amount of fatigue duty, and suffered hostility from whites who opposed or resented the very idea of black soldiers and their white officers.

Settling In

Those former slaves who presented themselves at the Union camp in La Grange, Tennessee, in March 1864 typified many who left farms and plantations for the army. They wore a close-fitting wool shirt, homespun brown pantaloons too short in the legs and hanging loosely about the waist, maybe something on their feet, and perhaps a slouch hat. Colonel Robert Cowden, commanding officer of the 59th USCT at La Grange, wrote that the children of the black enlistees, "did not, together, have enough clothing on them to wad a shot-gun." They walked into camp with a "rolling, dragging, moping gait."[1] Life in camp for the new recruits began with receiving a haircut, a bath, and a uniform.

From 1863 on, black troops, having come under federal control, wore the same uniform as whites. This had not always been the case. Recruits in Hunter's regiment wore red pants, which made them easy targets. The black troops reportedly hated them.[2] Well-intentioned white supporters of the 54th Massachusetts Volunteers pressed for uniforms of canary yellow and scarlet, believing that blacks, like children, favored bright colors. The standard federal blue uniform, in addition to being less conspicuous, signaled the beginning of the transformation of men with few rights and skills into American soldiers. Quartermasters issued each man in Cowden's regiment a dark blue dress coat, light blue trousers, an overcoat, two blue jackets (called blouses), a blue forage cap with black visor, and a pair of "gunboats," or rough, black shoes. Next, each recruit received a haversack (a large bag with one strap carried over the shoulder), in which he kept a cartridge box, blanket, bayonet, scabbard, mess kit (consisting of a canteen, knife, fork, tin cup, and plate), and a knapsack for personal items such as pen, razor, brush, soap, underclothing, needle, and thread.

Next came an infantryman's weapon and ammunition. Institutional bias against black troops within the War Department often dictated that black troops receive discarded weapons—arms of inferior quality to those issued whites. In keeping with their second-class status many black soldiers received an antiquated smooth-bore musket that lacked the range and accuracy of the standard-issue rifle that most white troops received, a circumstance that many commanders of the USCT considered unacceptable. Brigadier General William Birney, an Alabama-born abolitionist, complained in a letter to Major Charles W. Foster: "To put men into the field with poor weapons when it is known they will be massacred if they are whipped is little short of murder."[3] "Ammunition furnished to my command has been of the most worthless description," reported a colonel of the 1st U.S. Colored Cavalry (USCC). As late as April 1864, Adjutant General Lorenzo Thomas complained to Secretary of War Stanton that the USCT companies he inspected on Ship Island, Mississippi, had inferior weapons and should be issued Springfield muskets. According to Thomas, "This Regiment, like most of this class of soldiers, have the old flintlock muskets, altered to percussion, which have been in use for a long time. The muskets of this Regiment were condemned once, and have been condemned by an Inspector for a second time."[4]

To remedy the inadequacy of weapons provided them by the government, many black soldiers (defying regimental orders) brought personal weapons with them to camp. So many men in the 6th U.S. Colored Artillery, stationed at Natchez, Mississippi, in 1864, carried concealed pistols that the regiment's officers issued a ban and confiscated their weapons.

Like white troops, the men of the USCT also experienced mishaps with their government-issued weapons. "The men must be cautioned repeatedly," an officer of the 107th USCT remarked, "against the habit of snapping the hammers of Guns against the Cones [on which the percussion cap was placed]; which oftentimes renders the arm unserviceable." Officers also reported numerous cases of black soldiers mishandling capped and loaded weapons or firing their weapons in camp, especially at night. "Too much attention cannot be paid by the men in handling their arms," wrote the commander of the 59th USCT. "So much unnecessary suffering has been caused by the careless manner in which so many soldiers have heretofore handled their arms."[5]

Black cavalry regiments also experienced problems with their equipage. When white troops lost thousands of horses during Grant's May 1864 Wilderness Campaign, officers ordered members of the 1st USCC to surrender their horses to white units. Cavalry officers assigned to black cavalry troops scrounged government corrals to procure "a sufficient number of old hacks, horses, and mules . . . deemed fit only for drill practice, and with no thought of taking the field with them."[6] Black cavalrymen also suffered from insufficient and inferior provisions. An officer of the 3rd USCC reported that the men's hard tack "was so wormy that they could not eat it."[7]

The ex-slaves who flocked into camp in Gallatin, Tennessee, in November 1863, experienced yet other obstacles. There they found Colonel Thomas J. Morgan organizing the 14th USCT. With no experienced noncommissioned officers (all had just recently been promoted from the ranks), Morgan found it difficult "to evoke order out of chaos." The soldiers lacked tents. They lived "in an old filthy tobacco warehouse, where they fiddled, danced, sang, swore or prayed, according to their mood." With A. H. Dunlap, a clerk who had helped organize the 3rd USCT in Baltimore, at his side, Morgan started by examining each man "*a la Eden, sans* the fig leaves."[8] He rejected any enlistee with physical limitations. Though Morgan noted his recruits' inexperience, he commented favorably on the men's positive attitudes. "I know all about that," said one after hearing Morgan deliver a lengthy description of campaigning and fighting. "You may be killed in battle," Morgan continued. "Many a better man than me," the soldier replied, "has been killed in this war." Another responded to Morgan's warning about the risks of possibly dying in combat, "But my people will be free." Morgan concluded that "these men, though black in skin, had men's hearts and only needed right handling to develope [sic] into magnificent soldiers."[9]

While the new USCT recruits had to learn many things, including caring for their uniforms and firing their weapons, many, especially former slaves, had much deferential behavior to unlearn. In place of obsequiousness, real or feigned, it was essential that the black men learn the discipline and routine of the soldier and the military life. Taps put the men in Cowden's regiment to bed at nine, and the men learned, sometimes at the point of a bayonet, to stay in their tent until reveille the next morning. Free blacks who mobilized at Union camps in the North, such as at Ohio's Camp Delaware, Camp Meigs in Readville, Massachusetts, and Camp Stanton in Benedict, Maryland, usually arrived somewhat better educated and clothed than fugitive slaves who joined the USCT regiments in the South. U.S. Army officials believed that free blacks, though also accustomed to hard work, took longer to embrace the discipline of army life than ex-slaves, accustomed to harsh discipline on farms and plantations. Men of the USCT recruited in the North arrived in camps usually adequately staffed with officers to train and facilities to house and feed them.

The model training camp featured a grid pattern. Most of these camps positioned officers' quarters at the front and enlisted men's tents arranged in parallel lines to the rear. Between the officers' and the enlisted men's quarters stood the hospital, kitchen, stables, quartermaster's tent, and sutler's tent, where the proprietor, a civilian, sold, usually at high prices, such morsels as sardines, canned peaches, ginger cakes, condensed milk, and plug tobacco. Most camps sat near a creek or river to ensure an adequate supply of water. A ring of pickets stationed at the perimeter guarded USCT recruitment camps.

Camp William Penn, the largest training facility for black troops, ranked among the best. The camp overlooked Pennsylvania's cultivated rolling countryside, through which ran many creeks. The depot of the North Pennsylvania Railroad sat a mere half mile away, allowing easy travel between the camp and Philadelphia. The military installation consisted of neat rows of shelter tents (wedge-shaped two- or three-piece enclosures with wider panels at each end) for the recruits and wall or cabin tents (canvas enclosures with four vertical walls) for officers set on streets. Recruits wishing to take reading and writing classes did so in a large tent where members of a missionary society provided instruction. A parade ground behind the camp allowed ample room for recruits to drill and display for visitors their mastery of maneuvers and precision marching. "The stay at Camp William Penn," according to Major Benjamin W. Thompson, "was a very bright spot in my army experience. We were just in the suburbs of Philadelphia and went into the city often. . . . Our service with colored men made us heroes to our good Quaker friends."[10] The nearly 400 officers and 10,940 troops mobilized at the camp under the direction of Colonel Louis Wagner, a German-born veteran of the Second Battle of Bull Run, went on to distinguish themselves in such campaigns as Petersburg, Chaffin's Farm, and Fort Fisher.

From Recruit to Soldier

A uniform, a weapon, and a tent do not a soldier make. Not until he internalized the values, attitudes, and behaviors of the soldier did a recruit become a soldier. Officers used various methods to accomplish this goal. Colonel Higginson thought the best route to an orderly camp and combat readiness lay in reeducating his recruits to unlearn what he considered their childlike, unquestioning deference to authority—traits that he identified with slavery. Higginson expected manliness, pride, and self-respect from his men. He impressed upon them that his orders, and those of other officers, derived from military code, not mere whim. Higginson pointed out that he too had superiors, including Generals Saxton and Hunter.

To transform the ex-slaves into soldiers, Higginson replaced his men's demeaning red pants with blue ones, committed himself to instill in his men pride, a sense of self-worth, esprit de corps, and identification with Lincoln's army. Higginson, however, refused to make his soldiers into men as though they were the clay and he the potter. Instead, assisted by other officers, chaplains, nurses, and officers' wives, he succeeded in transforming escaped slaves into soldiers by replacing the brutish environment of slavery with the order, rigors, and routine of military life. Higginson forbade his men from talking with him, or any officer, with their caps off. (Slaves had often been required to remove their hats when conversing with a master or overseer.) Soldiers sa-

Military training introduced black soldiers to the same discipline whites experienced in the institutional effort to "make soldiers" of civilians. Apparently found guilty of some army infraction, these privates sit uncomfortably—perhaps for hours—on the equivalent of sawhorses, a punishment soldiers naturally called "riding the horse." Prints and Photographs Division, Library of Congress.

luted their officers, who returned the salute. Uniforms and equipage were to be kept clean and buttons polished. Guard duty, which soldiers performed in turns, gave men authority and responsibility unimaginable as slaves. Posted around the perimeter of the camp with a musket and entrusted with allowing into the camp only those who knew the password, pickets were instructed to shoot to kill any person who attempted to enter camp without giving the password. Military duties and performance, not skin color, dictated behavior. Higginson put to rest the worries of many soldiers by settling their wives and children in temporary housing near the camp.

By all accounts his regiment, the 1st South Carolina Volunteers, maintained a high level of morale, and the men acquitted themselves admirably in their many raids along the rivers and creeks of coastal South Carolina, culminating in their January 1863 raid up the Saint Marys River, on the Georgia-Florida border.

Other officers liberally employed rewards and punishments to train black troops under their command. For example, when a company of soldiers completed guard duty at Camp William Penn, the men gathered at a central point and fired their muskets at a target. The soldier with the best shot received a two-day pass. Anyone whose weapon did not discharge served four more hours of guard duty. Colonel Cowden held monthly drill competitions among the companies in his regiment. The company with the best performance, as judged by officers from another regiment, received a rosette, a small medal, to be worn on the left breast of their dress parade jackets. Such rewards reinforced lessons learned in drill and bolstered a company's pride and esprit de corps.

Some officers, however, relied on harsher measures to train their black troops. These included pistol whippings, verbal threats, blows with the flat of a sword or fist, or hanging a man by his thumbs. Joseph Holloway, a former slave from Mississippi, complained to Governor Andrew that "a parcel of coperhad [copperhead] orfices [officers] . . . drive us worse than ever the secash [secessionists] did." Holloway said he would rather be "back home with my boss [Confederate General James Pettigrew] than to be in any such a mess as this."[11]

In one instance a frustrated USCT officer lost his temper with a soldier struggling to load and fire his rifle. The officer called the soldier "a wooly headed nincompoop," aimed his gun for him one more time, and said he would kill the soldier if he did not load and discharge his weapon properly the next time. One officer spoke for many of his peers when he remarked, "I would rather swing a scythe all day than to endeavor to teach a squad of recruits any of the motions of the Manual of arms." More than one officer declared himself "ready to quit the business of teaching 'unbleached Americans.'"[12]

Such actions and comments underscored the value of carefully identifying and training white officers as undertaken by Foster, Webster, and Thomas. How officers selected noncommissioned officers constituted another important influence on the black troops' morale and performance.

The rank of sergeant was generally the highest rank to which men of color could aspire. However, white sergeants also served in the USCT. Some regimental commanders selected black noncommissioned officers based on observations and interviews with both candidates and the men under whom they would serve. As one such officer wrote to his family, "I have the honor and pleasure of appointing my non-commissioned officers. . . . I tell you they feel proud of it."[13] Other officers simply appointed noncommissioned officers on a trial-and-error basis. Perhaps not surprisingly, they found that repeated changes were required.

The 65th USCT presented an extreme example of selecting noncommissioned officers by the trial-and-error method. In one month officers demoted thirty-two noncommissioned officers and promoted others in their place. Needless to say, morale in the regiment suffered. Some officers took great pains helping black recruits to adapt to army life. Twice a year officers were required to read the Articles of War to their men. This twenty-one-page document, drawn from *The Regulations for the Army of the United States* (1861) and reprinted in the back of tactics manuals, described how soldiers were to conduct themselves. Knowing that few soldiers would learn much from an officer droning on and that limited reading skills prevented most recruits from studying the document themselves, many officers held regular meetings to explain and discuss, in language that the black soldiers understood, the regulations as well as the punishments for infractions.

For example, a soldier absent from camp without leave might be "bucked and gagged" for two hours. A soldier so punished sat with a gag in his mouth and his knees raised and arms outstretched. A thin log passed under his knees and over his elbows; rope tied his hands and ankles so that he could not move. A soldier guilty of talking back to a guard would be forced to stand on a barrel for a day. Deserters faced the most serious punishment of all: execution. "Our old masters would get angry with us and sometimes punish us almost to death, and we not understand why," remarked a black trooper. "But here if we are punished, we know why for the officers tell us our duty and never punish us unless we disobey."[14]

Ignorance of regulations could prove fatal. For example, a court-martial board sentenced Sergeant William Walker of the 21st USCT to execution by firing squad for his "mutiny" in November 1863 in protesting unequal pay. The sergeant pleaded that "never, since the organization of the company, have the 'Articles of War' been read to us nor any part of the 'Regulations' even."[15] His excuse proved to be of no avail. The army executed Walker on March 1, 1864.

In another case, a company in the 49th USCT stacked its arms in protest over their captain searching their tents and throwing away such personal items as candles. Writing to Secretary of War Stanton, a black soldier explained that the men just sought improved treatment from their commander and that "at the time of doing this we were not aware what the consequences of Mutiny would be."[16] The court-martial board, finding no culpability on the part of the officers for failing to inform the men about the consequences of their actions, sentenced two men to death and seventeen others to life sentences and ordered one to wear a ball and chain for the rest of his military service.

USCT officers also received punishments for misconduct—demonstrating that fairness prevailed in the ranks. After an inquiry found a major guilty of cowardice, his commanding officer ripped off the man's buttons, broke his sword, tore off his insignia, and had him driven out of camp in an oxcart to the tune of "Rogue's March." The entire regiment witnessed the ex-officer's public humiliation. Seeing an officer cashiered served to convince those who observed the defrocking that officers would also be held accountable for their actions. Morale and readiness deteriorated when officers escaped punishment. This occurred in the 38th USCT when officers withheld bounty payments, extracted loans from enlisted men they did not pay back, and charged exorbitant rates for tobacco and for repairing watches.

Learning the Work of Soldiering

The lion's share of the black soldier's training consisted of constant drill. A soldier at Ohio's recruitment facility at Camp Delaware near Columbus started his day with reveille at 5:00 a.m., then an hour of drill followed by breakfast and policing the camp. Then he returned to drill until lunchtime. The trooper spent the rest of the day in battalion drill. After dinner he took part in an evening dress parade and was in bed by 9:30 p.m. Drill continued to be an important part of a USCT soldier's routine once he left training camp and entered the field. A typical day for the 54th Massachusetts Volunteers stationed in South Carolina consisted of reveille at 5:00 a.m., followed by drill from 5:30 to 9:00 a.m., with yet more drill from 4:00 to 6:00 p.m. and dress parade at 6:30 p.m. Men spent the rest of the day cleaning their equipage, studying, sleeping, eating, and policing camp.

Drill taught men to maneuver as a unit and to load and fire their weapons.

Troops learned to execute commands for such activities as "forward march," "double-time," "right face," and "left face." A regiment in battle might, for instance, be required on command to change its formation from a column (four men abreast and two-hundred fifty deep) to a rank-and-file formation (five hundred men wide and two men deep) or vice versa. Because these and other maneuvers might well decide the outcome of an engagement, regiments had to execute them with precision. Drill also contributed to building esprit de corps among companies and regiments that were mostly made up of soldiers who did not know one another before enlisting. Rain and snow provided no respite from the repetition of drilling and practicing the manual of arms.

The black troops learned to listen first to preparatory commands and then commands of execution. In order to "march," for instance, the officer first addressed the unit, as "Squad," set the pace of movement with "Common time," and then issued the execution command, "March." In 1863 the War Department issued a tactical manual, *U.S. Infantry Tactics, for the Instruction, Exercise, and Manoeuvres, of the Soldier, a Company, Line of Skirmishers, and Battalion; for the Use of the Colored Troops of the United States Infantry* that specified the correct responses to the orders. It stated, for example,

> At the first command, the recruit will throw the weight of the body on the right leg, without bending the left knee. . . . At the third command, he will smartly, but without a jerk, carry straight forward the left foot twenty-eight inches from the right, the sole near the ground, the ham extended, the toe a little depressed, and, as also the knee, slightly turned out; he will, at the same time, throw the weight of the body forward, and plant flat the left foot, without shock, precisely at the distance where it finds itself from the right when the weight of the body is brought forward, the whole of which will now rest on the advanced foot. The recruit will next, in like manner, advance the right foot and plant it as above, the heel twenty-eight inches from the heel of the left foot, and thus continue to march without crossing legs, or striking the one against the other, without turning the shoulders, and preserving always the face direct to the front.[17]

Many white observers complimented black troops at drill, judging their performance equal to, or better than, that of white units, though the explanations of some white observers for this proficiency missed the mark.

Writing from Chattanooga, Tennessee, during the winter of 1865, a *Man-*

chester Guardian reporter condescendingly chalked up black troops' mastery of drill to a combination of qualities allegedly common to the former slave. These included his natural docility, which "makes him, when under a proper master, attentive and obedient; his strong devotional feelings and love of parade . . . [and] his love of music and appreciation of time (as evidenced by his dancing abilities)." The journalist noted, however, that one of the purported qualities allowing former slaves to excel at drill—docility—hindered the black recruit's development as a soldier. "The fact of his having for generations been cowed . . . give him," the newspaperman continued, "a habitual if not instinctive dread of the white man as an opposing force." Once a soldier overcame his sense of dread, this reporter envisioned "no reason why coloured troops cannot be made as effective as white troops."[18] The journalist's observations reflected the conventional wisdom of the day among whites regarding the influence of slavery on black behavior and character.

In May 1863 a white officer from General Daniel Ullmann's brigade of black troops in Baton Rouge, Louisiana, heaped praise, without analysis, on one of the regiments. In his opinion "They drill[ed] far better than any white troops I have ever seen. . . . They made no mistakes or confusion. . . . We all came away delighted, and many said that they had changed their minds entirely in regard to the intelligence and capability of improvement in the 'nigger.'"[19]

Like white soldiers, the black troops repeatedly practiced with their weapons in various formations. Officers worked with new recruits showing them how to hold their rifles, how to sight targets, and how best to load, aim, and squeeze the trigger.

A common rifle drill consisted of nine men in each of three rows, one directly behind the other. Each row of men in turn loaded, aimed, and fired their weapons until each row could comfortably fire three shots in sixty seconds. The training officer fired his pistol in the air while another shouted obscenities to simulate battle conditions. One officer designed a system that gave soldiers immediate feedback on their marksmanship. He placed a six-foot-high, twenty-two-inch-wide frame, across which he stretched a sheet with a bull's-eye in the middle, two hundred yards from the firing line. A man stood in a trench directly in front of the target and deep enough to conceal him. Using a stick with a flag on one end to call for a cease fire and a disk on the other, the spotter placed the disk next to the hole created by each shot to show the soldier where his round pierced the target.

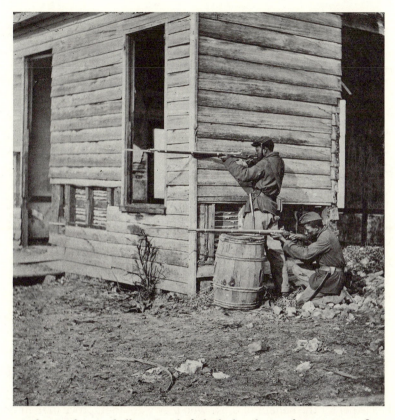

Slave codes in the antebellum South forbade bondsmen from owning firearms. Recruits here concentrate on use of the rifled musket—and learn to take available cover. Prints and Photographs Division, Library of Congress.

Social and Religious Support

Black troops learned more than how to march and fire a weapon, however. Many entered the service illiterate and exited having learned to read and write. To an extent the Union army itself served as a schoolhouse in which white and black chaplains, along with white officers and military wives, taught the men of the USCT. The act of learning how to read—formerly outlawed by the southern slave codes—empowered Lincoln's black troops as soldiers and as men. First Sergeant John Sweney of the 13th USCT, born a Kentucky slave, believed that literacy was essential in preparing the black soldiers to become good citizens, leaders, and businessmen following the war. "We as soldeirs [sic]," he wrote, "have our officers who are our protection To teach how us [sic] to act and to do But Sir what we want is a general system of education In our regiment for our moral and literary elevation."[20]

The men of the USCT thirsted for education. As soldiers they no longer had to learn to read surreptitiously. In the span of four months one black regiment raised $700 to buy school supplies and to pay for their own teachers and donated $60 to help fund a black school in a neighboring town. The 7th USCT established a school for its noncommissioned officers, who in turn taught the men in their companies. When stationed at Camp Nelson, Kentucky, Duty Sergeant Elijah Marrs and Sergeant Major George Thomas of the 12th U.S. Colored Heavy Artillery conducted classes among the recruits, teaching them vocal music and the rudiments of English grammar.

At the urging of black chaplains such as the Reverend Henry McNeal Turner of the 1st USCT, the government furnished spelling books and teachers for soldiers who wanted to read. Many learned basic literacy in camp in informal schools, where literate blacks provided evening study sessions for their comrades. In September 1864 the Reverend John R. Bowles, chaplain of the 55th Massachusetts Volunteer Regiment, reported to General Lorenzo Thomas that the Christian Commission Society had amply supplied him with religious tracts and newspapers. "There are some who cannot read and write," Bowles wrote Thomas, and "we have opened an evening school in the chapel for the benefit of those who may work to improve in their education." In another report Chaplain Bowles informed Thomas that morals among the blacks in his regiment were improving steadily. "Cursing, which was almost universal, is now heard less frequent[ly]. Card playing, and other amusements, are decreasing as the men find better and more useful ways of spending their leisure moments. Cases of gross immorality are not very frequent, owing to the strict enforcement of good discipline, and the absence of temptation."[21] As Bowles's report suggests, the black troops quickly identified a direct connection between literacy, clean living, freedom, leadership, and full manhood that emancipated them from the bonds of ignorance and equalized them with whites.

Susie King Taylor, born a slave in 1842 in Savannah, Georgia, taught many of the men in Higginson's 1st South Carolina Volunteers. A friend of her grandmother's had taught Taylor how to read and write. She and her brother arrived at the woman's house at nine each morning with their books "wrapped in paper to prevent the police or white persons from seeing them."[22] In Georgia at that time, any black person teaching another black person to read or write could be fined or whipped. During the Civil War Taylor worked as a laundress to Company E, in which her husband served as a sergeant. Taylor instructed the men in her spare time.

Officers' wives, like Mrs. Frances Beecher, wife of Colonel James Beecher, commander of the 35th USCT, also taught the black soldiers. Beecher's regiment operated in the Carolinas and Florida. The regiment's chaplain and several officers often assisted Mrs. Beecher in her efforts. During their scarce free time the soldiers often huddled around a spelling book, a primer, a missionary society tract, or a Bible. In light of the fact that most soldiers could only sign their name with an "X" when they enlisted, Mrs. Beecher took pride in the fact that when they were discharged from the 35th, each man in the regiment could sign his name.

Colonel Cowden of the 59th USCT built a schoolhouse that the regiment's chaplain and his wife staffed. Wives and children, as well as soldiers, were welcome to attend. The school served as a chapel on Sundays for Bible study and Sunday school.

Soldiers, however, did not limit their learning to the classroom. They studied on duty, as Chaplain Edwin Wheeler of the 80th USCT noted, and "regarded their books as an indispensable portion of their equipment." The "spelling book and the cartridge-box are generally attached to the same belt."[23]

The soldiers' appetite for learning impressed their teachers. Thomas Johnson, superintendent of schools for the 25th Army Corps, marveled that the men would use their free time for study. They "would draw from their pocket their treasured book and earnestly study its pages," Johnson said.[24] "I have been several years a teacher," Chaplain George S. Barnes of the 29th USCT reported, "but have never witnessed a stronger desire to learn or know more rapid progress."[25]

Army regulations required each Union regiment to have an ordained Christian minister as a chaplain. Most were white. Only fourteen black chaplains served during the war. The War Department required chaplains to report to the regiment's colonel at the end of each quarter on the moral and religious condition of the regiment and to suggest improvements. Governor Andrew of Massachusetts had more specific expectations for William Jackson and William Grimes, the chaplains he appointed to his state's black infantry regiments. The clergymen, Andrew said, should communicate "the ideas and sentiments of Christian duty . . . [and] help the men become good soldiers, . . . an honor to Massachusetts and a means of elevating the position of the people of color hereafter."[26]

Chaplains in USCT regiments held various responsibilities. The men expected them to be their confidants, to visit them in hospitals, to listen to their tales of homesickness, to boost them up when their courage faltered, and to support their opposition to slavery, write letters, circulate hometown newspapers, and encourage relatives to send food, money, and books. Chaplains gathered men together in their free time for religious services. They counseled men awaiting execution. Chaplain Garland White, while comforting Private Samuel Mapp of the 10th USCT, who had attempted to kill his captain, "'cited in plain terms the case of the dying thief' on the cross beside the Lord's on Calvary." These words, White said, gave Mapp hope.[27]

Chaplains often praised black soldiers' actions in articles they wrote for newspapers, especially the African Methodist Episcopal Church's weekly newspaper, the *Christian Recorder*. For example, the Reverend White described men not complaining about being assigned to lay in rifle pits filled with water. He assured readers that soldiers who had made the ultimate sacrifice—dying for the Union cause—had achieved salvation as heroes fighting valiantly for hearth and home. The Reverend Turner wrote of the 1st USCT's valiant charge against the Confederates at Petersburg: "The bayonets were fixed, and away went Uncle Sam's sable sons across an old field nearly three quarters of a mile wide, in the face of rebel grape and canister and the unbroken clatter of thousand of muskets."[28]

Officers also expected chaplains in USCT regiments to assist in recruiting and enabling soldiers to adapt to army life. Those chaplains who succeeded best relied, in addition to theological training, on their personal qualities, including large doses of charisma, magnetism, and resourcefulness.

Colonels in USCT regiments also commonly employed women, other than officers' wives, as nurses, teachers, and laundresses. Most commanders, like Colonel James Williams of the 79th USCT, banned "unauthorized intruders, especially 'lewd women,'" from camp. Such females, Williams believed, undermined soldiers' morals and good order. Accordingly, he forbade any soldier "from harboring women."[29] A first-time offender lost a month's pay that went to a black school near the camp. A repeat offender spent a month at hard labor without pay.

Black women in communities throughout the North supported their

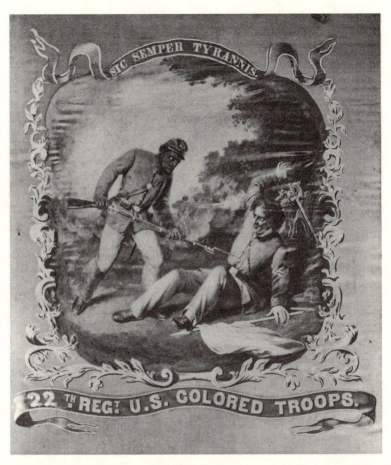

Each USCT regiment proudly carried colors in parade and battle. This design, the work of the African American artist David Bustill Bowser, appeared on the flag of the 22nd USCT. In a truly pointed gesture, it adopted the motto of the state of Virginia, "Sic Semper Tyrannis" (Thus Always to Tyrants) but put the slaveholder in the position of the vanquished, or soon to be vanquished, enemy of liberty. Prints and Photographs Division, Library of Congress.

troops at the front. They formed women's auxiliaries. The Ladies Association for the Relief of the Sick and Wounded (Colored) Soldiers of New York donated money, food, clothes (especially undergarments), and other goods, as did the Ladies of the Twelfth Baptist Church (Boston), the Ladies Aid Society (Norwich, Connecticut), and the Visiting Committee of Mrs. Keckley's Contraband Relief Society (Washington, D.C.). From London, England, Ellen Craft, the famous runaway Georgia slave, coauthor of *Running a Thousand*

Miles for Freedom (1860), and slave expatriate, sent hand-sewn clothing to black soldiers.

The women's auxiliaries raised money to pay for regimental flags and banners. The Colored Ladies' Union Relief Association proudly presented a banner to General Wild's brigade when it left New Bern, North Carolina, in July 1863. The regimental flag of the First District Colored Volunteers, portraying the Goddess of Liberty handing a musket to a black soldier while resting one foot on the head of a serpent, was financed by the fund-raising of women in the nation's capital. The War Department gave black women an official role in the war effort on January 16, 1864, when it authorized United States General Hospitals to hire them as cooks or nurses at the rate of ten dollars a month and one daily ration.

Demoralizing Effect of Fatigue Duty

The exorbitant amount of fatigue duty assigned to the USCT by their officers blunted, to some degree, the morale-boosting actions of chaplains, women, sympathetic commanders, War Department officials, and even President Lincoln. Reflecting the racial attitudes of white Americans generally, many officers considered blacks better suited than whites to labor and perform menial duties. Though they doubted the black man's ability to fight, they credited him with an alleged immunity to tropical diseases and a belief that those with black skin and African heritage fared better than whites doing hard work in the South's hot climate. They also believed that Lincoln favored mobilizing black troops as support troops in order to free whites for combat.

In February 1863, following the eruption of tensions between white and black regiments in the Department of the Gulf stationed at Ship Island, a *New York Times* reporter made the case for limiting black soldiers to fatigue duty. Quoting the section of Lincoln's final Emancipation Proclamation that referred to black troops "garrisoning forts and positions," the journalist predicted that it would require time for "traits of character that have been dormant for generations" to emerge among the ex-slaves before they could be trusted in battle. Eventually, he explained, "Our . . . [white] soldiers will be glad enough to have this work taken off their hands by the acclimated negroes."[30]

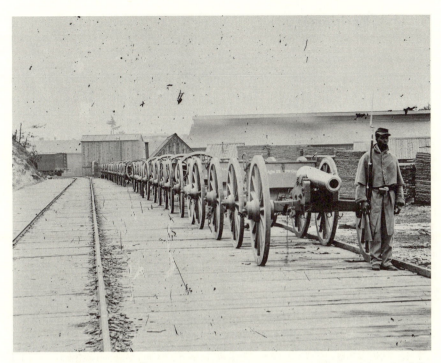

Offering an illustration of "fatigue" or noncombat duty, a black soldier dutifully guards a string of artillery pieces and accompanying equipment at City Point, Virginia. Civil War Glass Negative Collection, Library of Congress.

Because officials in Washington and in combat zones shared the newspaperman's opinions, the USCT often seemed destined to do little more than construct fortifications, dig trenches, load and unload supply wagons and ships, and guard interior supply and railroad lines. White officers routinely assigned black troops the least desirable menial assignments, including emptying latrines and ship bunkers and then, as historian Ira Berlin explains, "cursed them for doing the odious work." "Instead of the musket," Nimrod Rowley of the 20th USCT complained, "it is the spad and the Whelbarrow and the Axe cuting in one of the most horable swamps in Louisiana stinking and misery Men are Call to go on thes fatiuges wen sum of them are scarc[e] Able to get Along." Another black infantryman, Thomas D. Freeman of the 54th Massachusetts, grumbled that "we are not Soldiers but Labourers working for Uncle Sam for nothing but our board and clothes. . . . It is nothing but work from morning till night Building Batteries Hauling Guns Cleaning Bricks clearing up land for other Regiments to settle on. . . . Now do you call this Equality if so God help such Equality."[31]

In June 1864 Adjutant General Lorenzo Thomas ordered commanders in the Mississippi valley to distribute fatigue duties equitably. Not all officers complied, however. Thomas noted in his November 7, 1864, report to Stanton: "Where white and black troops come together in the same command the latter have to do the work. At first this was always the case, and in vain did I endeavor to correct it, contending that if they were to be made soldiers, time should be afforded for drill and discipline, and that they should only have their fair share of fatigue duty."[32] Stanton apparently never responded to Thomas's complaint.

Recreation

Despite long days of drill punctuated by fatigue duty, black troops nonetheless found time for recreation when officers relaxed their discipline and left the men to their own devices. Their off-duty activities allowed the men of the USCT "to consolidate their freedom and negotiate significant social changes." In camp, some devoted their pastime hours to "polishing brass buttons, brushing uniforms, and blacking boots." Others, beyond the watchful eye of their white commissioned and black noncommissioned officers, prayed, sang, played musical instruments, swapped stories, gambled, debated, wrote letters, and published camp newspapers. In these activities they asserted themselves, building group identity, social cohesion, and loyalty, and sustained morale. While playing games and engaging in various modes of cultural expression, while eating and drinking, and while praying, the men of the USCT reflected upon the meaning of such essential concepts as citizenship, democracy, duty, freedom, honor, loyalty, and patriotism.[33]

The men liked to gamble, eat, and drink in their tents. They feasted on fresh peaches, strawberries, and other fruits bought on payday at the sutler's tent. Like soldiers throughout history, the men of the USCT entertained "ladies of the night" when they were able to avoid their officers' scrutiny. The men of the USCT also consumed liquor to ward off boredom and enhance camaraderie with their fellows. Many a soldier overindulged in "demon rum," forcing some officers to ban alcohol from camp entirely.

But by far the black troops' favorite pastime consisted of gathering, exchanging stories, and singing around the campfire. White soldiers of course also congregated and sang around campfires. They tended to sing popular songs extolling patriotism, courage, and loved ones back home. The men of the USCT, however, often sat near a fire and reflected more on their future than on their past. They commonly improvised songs in the call-and-response mode common to African American music of the time.

The song "I Know Moon-Rise " reproduced in part below, spoke to their hopes and dreams. A single "deep rich voice" started with

I know moon-rise, I know star-rise.

Others then repeated the refrain:

To lay dis body down.

The leader then called:

I walk in de moonlight, I walk in de starlight,

and half a dozen took up the refrain:

To lay dis body down.

The leader then called:

I'll walk in de graveyard, I'll walk through de graveyard. . . .

Then fifty voices joined in with

Lay dis body down
I go to de judgement in de evenin' of de day,
When I lay dis body down
And my soul and your soul will meet in de day
When I lay dis body down.

A white officer judged the men's voices "a Creation chorus." Another praised the songs sung by the men of the USCT and "the vocal expression of the simplicity of their faith and the sublimity of their long resignation."[34]

5 How Black Troops Gained the Glory and Paid the Price

THOUGH BLACK SOLDIERS entered combat as early as October 29, 1862, when the 1st Kansas Colored Volunteers engaged the enemy at Island Mound, Missouri, and fought valiantly at Port Hudson (May 1863), Milliken's Bend (June 1863), and Fort Wagner (July 1863), by spring 1864, many whites nonetheless still doubted if they would fight and, if so, fight well. Armies reflect the ethos of the societies they serve, and the discrimination that the men of the USCT experienced—in pay, duties, equipment, medical care—mirrored that experienced by people of color in white America at large. In 1864 the USCT would be tested in new ways. The men knew that if captured by the enemy they faced enslavement or an even worse fate—murder at the hands of the Rebels.

Massacres and Revenge

The most infamous incident of the Confederates' murderous policy occurred at the battle of Fort Pillow, Tennessee, on April 12, 1864. Fort Pillow stood on bluffs high above the Mississippi River near Henning, Tennessee, forty miles north of Memphis. In January 1863 a force under Confederate Major General Nathan Bedford Forrest had captured five Union gunboats on the Cumberland River near Nashville. They stripped the black sailors naked, tied them to trees, liberally applied the lash, and left them to starve. More than a year later, Forrest, a former wealthy planter and slave trader, with around fifteen hundred troops overpowered Fort Pillow's small federal garrison. Only three USCT companies and a company of white Tennessee Unionists, totaling about six hundred men, defended the Union fort.

The historical record remains unclear. Forrest either ordered the massacre or lost control of his men, who proceeded to murder Fort Pillow's defenders well into the night after they had surrendered. Either way, Forrest, who after the Civil War became the first Grand Wizard of the Ku Klux Klan, may not have cared about the fate of the almost three hundred dead black and white Yankees.

In a letter to his sisters, a Confederate soldier, Sergeant Achilles V. Clark, depicted the ugly slaughter: "The poor deluded negroes would run up to our men fall on their knees and with uplifted hands scream for mercy but they were ordered to their feet and then shot down."[1] "I saw at least ten soldiers shot individually, with white handkerchiefs over their heads," Edward H. Benton, a civilian who owned land near the fort, told a military investigator. "They tore off pieces of their shirts—anything they could get." Benton's testimony, which appeared in the *New York Daily Tribune*, documented that Forrest's men shot nearly all of the black troops after they had surrendered. Some reportedly were buried alive.[2] A Rebel private, incensed that white Union soldiers fought alongside blacks, shot one white trooper dead in the head as he lay in bed in a makeshift hospital near the scene of the massacre.

Less than a week after the Fort Pillow butchery, on April 18, Confederate forces overwhelmed the 1st and 2nd Kansas Colored Infantry on an expedition to gather corn at Poison Springs, Arkansas, 120 miles southwest of Little Rock. Rebel soldiers killed all wounded and captured African American troops. Confederates competed with each other to see who could crush the most heads by driving their wagons over the heads of the wounded and dead Union troops lying in the field. They also scalped and stripped the bodies of three white officers.

Men of the USCT suffered similar cruelties in southern prisons. Dr. George Rogers Clark Todd, a brilliant Confederate surgeon and a brother of Abraham Lincoln's wife, Mary Todd Lincoln, repeatedly mistreated USCT captives at the prison in Charleston, South Carolina. He ordered black troops to be whipped, for example, for speaking to a white Union officer or for fending off a white deserter's attempt to steal a washbasin belonging to a USCT soldier.

The Fort Pillow massacre created national headlines and called attention to the conditions under which black soldiers fought and died. Abolitionists and other friends of the USCT called for Lincoln's administration to avenge the murder of the men who were killed as they tried to surrender.

For example, writing to Secretary of War Stanton, Theodore Hodgkins, a black New Yorker, demanded that the U.S. Army retaliate against the Confederates. Until Fort Pillow, Hodgkins wrote, the government had shrouded the "slaughters of colored troops" in "a sort of secrecy." But the cold-blooded execution of black troops "gives the government an opportunity to show the world whether the rebels or the U.S. have the strongest power." Should Lincoln's administration not seek immediate revenge (Hodgkins proposed the mass execution of an equal number of Confederate prisoners of war), "it may as well disband *all its colored troops* for no soldiers whom the government will not protect can be depended upon." Hodgkins insisted that he did not base his proposal on vindictiveness but made it "in the interest of my poor suffering confiding fellow negros."[3]

Black troops also sought revenge. On April 30, 1864, at Jenkins Ferry on the Saline River in Grant County, Arkansas, the 2nd Kansas Colored Infantry evened the score. After beating back Confederate infantry attacks, one company of black Jayhawkers stayed behind while the rest of the regiment moved on toward Little Rock. A Confederate soldier, John H. Lewis of the 18th Texas Infantry, wounded with a bullet in his leg, saw from behind a tree stump where he had taken cover the grisly scene that unfolded in front of him. "The firing ceased and our army was gone. Soon I looked around and saw some black negroes cutting our wounded boys' throats," Lewis confided to his diary.[4] He crawled farther back into the woods.

In a similar episode, sixty troops from the 6th U.S. Colored Artillery surprised a band of guerillas outside of Vidalia, Louisiana, on May 5, 1864, where they "fought like demons, making no effort to take prisoners." A correspondent for the *Philadelphia Inquirer* believed this action to be "the first act of retaliation for the barbarities of Fort Pillow."[5]

These and other retaliations caused Confederate president Jefferson Davis to reconsider his stated policy of executing and enslaving captured black troops and executing their white officers. Reports surfaced in May 1864 of

Confederate surgeons treating black troops' wounds to convince the men of the USCT that they could surrender safely and thereby end retaliatory murders. In March 1864, Davis had ordered his commanders to keep captured black soldiers alive, not because of any concern for the black troops, but rather to reduce the number of Rebel fatalities. Confederates imprisoned men of the USCT in, among other prisons, Georgia's notorious Andersonville Prison. The Rebels put prisoners who were well enough to work replacing and repairing prison walls and burying the one hundred soldiers a day who died at Andersonville. The black prisoners assigned to the burial detail received barely enough rations and fresh water to enable them to labor. Among the Union prisoners of war at Andersonville were two white officers of the USCT. Had they commanded white troops, the Confederates would have incarcerated them in the officer prison at nearby Macon, Georgia.

Black Troops on the Offensive

The men of the USCT fought in 449 separate fights, mostly in minor engagements and skirmishes. They did, however, participate in a number of offensives. When black troops went on the attack they tended to punch holes in the Rebels' lines. Many white officers believed that ferocity, fueled by a desire to prove their manhood and patriotism while knowing the consequences if captured, was the black soldier's strongest asset. As one officer wrote to his wife, "I confess I am surprised at the dash and courage of these men. I have never felt *sure* of them before and even now I fear they would not have that steadiness under fire that many have but for a charge they cannot be beat."[6]

Black troops' first major assault occurred at the Rebel stronghold of Port Hudson, Louisiana, on the Mississippi River on May 27, 1863. By the spring of 1863 Union forces controlled the river except for the stretch between Vicksburg and Port Hudson. While General Ulysses S. Grant besieged Vicksburg, General Nathaniel P. Banks attempted to dislodge the Confederates from Port Hudson. There, on the morning of May 27 the 1st and 3rd Louisiana Native Guards prepared to attack the formidable Confederate position. Both the Guards' provisional commander, General William Dwight, and a captain under his command, Pythagoras E. Holcomb of the 2nd Vermont Battery, had little commitment to or appreciation for the black troops under their command. In a letter to his family, Holcomb asked, "What's the use to have men from Maine, Vermont and Massachusetts dying down here in these swamps."

He continued, "You can't replace these men, but if a nigger dies, all you have to do is send out and get another one."[7] Dwight nevertheless assured Lieutenant Colonel Chauncey Bassett and Colonel John A. Nelson, commanders of the two Guards regiments, that their men would encounter smooth terrain and that support would be forthcoming if needed.

As these discussions occurred, sergeants lined the Guards up for roll call. Color Sergeant Anselmas Planciancois held the Guards' unfurled banner. The high-spirited soldiers promised themselves that they would take no Confederate prisoners in their assault on Port Hudson. They awaited orders to advance while two white regiments made the first assault. The white troops failed to penetrate the Rebels' defenses. At 10:00 a.m. eleven hundred black troops marched four abreast across Foster's Creek on a bridge built of india rubber pontoons. Once across the creek the men advanced in skirmish formation through woods on either side of Telegraph Creek. Soon they encountered not the promised smooth terrain but a swamp of cottonwoods, cypresses, and willows, thick underbrush, and unexpected gullies. Two hundred yards ahead stood bluffs manned by Confederate infantry and artillery. A stream of backwater from the river formed a moat between the bluff and any who dared to approach.

The Rebels struck first with a barrage of canister, shell, and rifle fire. Though the deadly enfilade opened gaps in the Union lines, the Guards closed up and pressed forward. They made at least three futile charges before both the men and their leaders realized that further fighting would be suicidal. A solid shot severed Sergeant Planciancois's head from his body. Only the cover of trees and stumps prevented a total massacre. To make matters worse, Dwight's promised support never materialized. Survivors retreated through waist-deep swamp water. Dwight, in a drunken stupor, ordered the retreating troops to charge yet again. But soberer heads prevailed, and the troops advanced no more.

When the smoke of battle had cleared, the Guards had suffered two hundred casualties; the Confederates escaped the battle with not a single casualty. The cease-fire called to allow Union troops to retrieve their dead and wounded from the field excluded the Guards. White soldiers removed the bodies of their fallen comrades from the battlefield the next day. Bodies of the dead Guards, however, rotted on the open ground for six weeks, until July 9, when the Confederates surrendered Port Hudson.

The Guards' fighting at Port Hudson lasted a little more than three hours, and their service garnered positive reviews. "The severe test to which they were subjected, and the determined manner in which they encountered the enemy, leaves upon my mind no doubt of their ultimate success," Banks reported to General Halleck.[8] An editorial in the *New York Times*, which earlier had proposed limiting black troops to fatigue duty, reported: "Those black soldiers had never before been in any severe engagement . . . . and were yet subjected to the most awful ordeal that even veterans ever have to experience. . . . The men, white or black, who will not flinch from that, will flinch from nothing."[9] The Native Guards so impressed General Daniel Ullmann that he wrote Stanton commending their "brilliant conduct." "I have talked with hundreds of them," Ullmann assured Stanton. "They know . . . that, if we are unsuccessful, they will be remanded to worse a slavery than before. They also have a settled conviction that if they are taken [alive], they will be tortured and hung."[10]

Ten days later Confederate major general Richard Taylor, a former brother-in-law of Jefferson Davis, led five thousand Confederates to strengthen the Rebels' positions around Port Hudson and Vicksburg. On June 7, a brigade of fifteen hundred of Taylor's men, commanded by Brigadier General Henry E. McCulloch, attacked five understrength black regiments (the 8th, 9th, 11th, and 13th Louisiana Infantry Regiments and the 1st Mississippi Infantry of African Descent) and the 23rd Iowa Volunteer Regiment at Milliken's Bend, Louisiana, twenty-five miles above Vicksburg. One of the five black units, the 1st Mississippi Infantry, had been in service only three weeks; the men had received their muskets one day before the battle. The 11th Louisiana Infantry had mustered in with the 1st Mississippi and had the relative advantage of having received its weapons, antiquated Belgian rifles, three weeks earlier. Newly appointed white officers struggled to distinguish one private from another. "Contrabands looked alike to the unsophisticated," said one.[11]

As the battle began, the inexperienced black troops allowed the Rebels to pour through gaps in their lines to reach the levee that Union forces had reinforced with heavy timbers and cotton bales. There the opposing troops engaged in hand-to-hand combat with gun butts and bayonets. The Yankees had the best of the fight until the Rebels gained a position on the west side of the levee. From there they mowed the blue-clad troops down with murderous fire. The white Iowans stampeded away from the fight while the black troops broke and retreated to the edge of the Mississippi. Fortuitously for the Union troops, two Union gunboats arrived to drive off McCulloch's men.

At battle's end, the black troops, with the help of the gunboats, held Milliken's Bend but at a horrific cost. Acting Rear Admiral David Dixon Porter, who arrived at the scene soon after the fight, recalled, "The dead negroes lined the ditch inside of the parapet, or levee, and most were shot on the top of the head."[12] The 9th Louisiana Infantry Regiment lost almost 45 percent of its men either killed or wounded on that bloody morning.

In his post-action report following the fight at Milliken's Bend, the Union commander of the District of Northeastern Louisiana described to his superiors the Confederates' assault on the defenses manned by the inexperienced USCT. It was "a most terrible hand to hand conflict, of several minutes duration, our men using the bayonet freely and clubbing their guns with fierce obstinacy, contesting every inch of ground, until the enemy succeeded in flanking them." The Rebels, Brigadier General Elias S. Dennis reported, directed their enfilade "chiefly to the officers, who fell in numbers." Dennis praised the bravery and gallantry of the enlisted men and officers of the USCT who fought at Milliken's Bend. "Not 'till they were overpowered, and forced by superior numbers, did our men fall back behind the bank of the river, at the same time pouring volley after volley into the ranks of the advancing enemy."[13]

A month later Colonel Robert Gould Shaw led the 54th Massachusetts Volunteer Regiment in its ill-fated attack on Fort Wagner in Charleston Harbor. Shaw's soldiers, like those of Bassett and Nelson at Port Hudson, went into combat with no chance of overcoming the Confederates' superior defensive position. Like their brothers at Port Hudson, the men of the 54th Massachusetts fought courageously, suffered heavy losses, and provided yet additional evidence that black soldiers could fight satisfactorily—even valiantly.

Not until February 20, 1864, at the Battle of Olustee, fifty miles west of Jacksonville, Florida, would black troops again be part of a major campaign. There black troops participated in the largest military campaign waged in Florida, long a source of pork, salt, beef, and sugar for General Lee's armies. By invading Florida, Lincoln's government hoped to disrupt the Rebels' supply chain, sever its railroad network, redirect cotton and timber to Union depots, and liberate thousands of slaves who in turn would enlist in the USCT. The president approved the foray into Florida with the presidential election less than a year away. In addition to the military objectives involved, he hoped that the Jacksonville expedition would restore Florida to the Union in time to allow a pro-Lincoln delegation to attend the Republican National Conven-

In the popular Northern newssheet *Harper's Weekly*, Thomas Nast portrayed the charge of USCT at the Battle of Milliken's Bend, Louisiana, June 7, 1863. Union victory there helped ensure the success of U. S. Grant's envelopment of Vicksburg, Mississippi, which surrendered on July 4, leaving the Union in control of the entire Mississippi River. *Harper's Weekly*, July 4, 1863.

tion. Under the provisions of Lincoln's December 8, 1863, Proclamation of Amnesty and Reconstruction (commonly called his Ten Percent Plan), any seceding state could be readmitted to the Union if 10 percent of its 1860 legal voters signed a loyalty oath and reconstituted a loyal state government.

Fifty-five hundred Union soldiers, including the 1st North Carolina Colored Infantry, the 8th USCT, recently arrived from Camp William Penn, and the 54th Massachusetts Volunteers, commanded by General Truman Seymour, easily captured Jacksonville on February 7, 1864. They continued westward with the goal of reaching Tallahassee but progressed no further than Olustee, in present-day Baker County, where five thousand Confederates who had marched south from Georgia intercepted them. The battle of Olustee, also known as Ocean Pond, began at noon on February 20. Once again many black soldiers arrived on the firing line ill-trained and unprepared. Only half of the 8th USCT had been instructed in loading their weapons prior to the battle, and most had little training in how to use them. Their drilling had emphasized parade-ground marches, not fighting. The black troops also lacked adequate food and entered the battle exhausted from their march from Jacksonville.

Their inexperience and fatigue showed once the battle started. As the bullets began to fly, many of the men of the USCT became confused and disoriented, driving them to curl to the ground, according to Lieutenant Oliver Norton of the 8th USCT, "like frightened sheep in a hailstorm."[14] The survivors retreated. The 54th Massachusetts, the only USCT regiment in the battle with significant combat experience, joined the fight. Its regimental band lined the side of a road and came forth with strains of "The Star-Spangled Banner," renewing the men's energy.

While the 54th Massachusetts quickly repelled a Rebel charge, the North Carolinians fared less well. Outmanned, they soon fell back in the face of unrelenting Confederate fire. Seymour ordered a retreat back to Jacksonville. Most observers noted that the men of the 8th USCT fought as well as could be expected given their lack of training and inexperience, and in no case did any of the black troops run from the fight. Captain John Hamilton of Battery E, 3rd U.S. Artillery, observed the 8th USCT in combat and remarked, "I did not see one of their officers or men who showed cowardice."[15] Critics, however, faulted Seymour, who in July 1863 had favored Shaw's troops making the first assault on Fort Wagner so as "to get rid of these niggers," for expecting too much of the two untried black regiments. When the smoke of battle had cleared, Florida remained a source of foodstuffs for the Confederates, and Lincoln did not get his Florida delegation to the 1864 Republican National Convention.

Olustee marked another battle where Rebel soldiers murdered captured black troops, though not as many as some Rebel officers would have preferred. "General Seamore's [sic] Army is made up largely of negroes . . . who have come to steal, pillage, run over the state and murder, kill and rape our wives, daughters, and sweethearts. Let's teach them a lesson. I shall not take any negro prisoners in this fight," a lieutenant colonel of the 2nd Florida Cavalry Regiment shouted to his men just before the fight.[16] Surprisingly, the Confederates murdered only a few wounded black soldiers after the battle. More would have been slaughtered had it not been for the actions of Dr. Alex P. Heichold, a white surgeon for the 8th USCT, and soldiers of the 54th Massachusetts. As the Union army started its retreat back to Jacksonville, Heichold insisted that wounded black soldiers be loaded into ambulances first and whites loaded last on a space-available basis. He explained that he knew what would happen to captured white troops but was not sure of the fate that awaited captured black soldiers. During the retreat a locomotive pulling boxcars full of injured white and black soldiers broke down ten miles west of Jacksonville, potentially leaving the wounded blacks vulnerable to the murderous inclinations of any pursuing Confederates. Men of the 54th, having just marched the fifty miles from the battlefield to Jacksonville without having eaten since before the fight, turned around and marched back to the train, gathered up ropes and vines, attached them to the engine, and pulled the entire train several miles until horses relieved them. Many captured black troops ended up in Andersonville.

Olustee, like Fort Pillow, was a low point in the USCT's history. Following the battle Captain James W. Grace of the 54th Massachusetts reported that in their forced retreat, the Union troops had to leave most of their dead and wounded on the field. "We were badly beaten that night, and the next day we kept falling back, until we reached Jacksonville." Determined nonetheless to accentuate the positive, Grace praised his regiment's valor and credited it with bringing honor to both itself and Boston. "All concede that no regiment fought like it." He also noted that Congress finally had voted to equalize the pay between white and black troops. "All we want now is more troops; with them we would go forward again and drive the rebels from the State."[17]

Farther north, at the Battle of the Crater in Virginia on July 30, 1864, a group of Union soldiers who had been miners in Pennsylvania volunteered to open the way for Grant to take Petersburg, Virginia, and then to move on to capture Richmond. They tunneled under a portion of the Confederate defenses, packed their excavation with black powder, and, after one failed attempt, detonated the powder kegs at 4:41 a.m. The explosion instantly killed 250 to 300 Confederates and created a crater 30 feet deep, 175 feet long, and 60 feet wide. Years later William Hannibal Thomas, a sergeant in Company I, 5th USCT, recalled observing the explosion of the mine and the resulting debacle at the crater. "I was in front of Petersburg Va," he recalled in 1911, "and witnessed the explosion of that mine. . . . It was a never to be forgotten sight of death and devastation." Thomas's unit supplied skirmishers on the extreme right of the charging 9th Corps, but during the battle Union commanders held most of the men of the 5th USCT in reserve.[18]

The original battle plan at the Crater called for black troops to rush into the break in the lines. At the last minute, however, Major General George G. Meade decided to lead the attack with white troops, reasoning that if the mission failed, critics could not allege that Meade needlessly expended black lives. As fate would have it, poorly trained white troops instead rushed into the crater, where they quickly found themselves trapped in its loose soil and steep slopes. The all-black 4th Division, commanded by Brigadier General Edward Ferrero, rushed in to support the white troops. Unable to counter the fierce fire of the Confederates, the men of the USCT, most experiencing their first combat and having already lost many of their officers, stalled. Many tried to retreat, but Confederate fire cut them down and prevented their withdrawal. The Rebels killed and wounded some nine hundred black troops, slamming their heads with musket butts and ramming their bodies with bayonets. Many had unsuccessfully tried to surrender.

Following the battle some criticized the black troops' performance, construing their move to the rear as evidence of cowardice. George F. Cram of the 105th Illinois Volunteer Regiment, a unit held in reserve during the battle, wrote his mother: "What a pity! When so near the most brilliant victory ever known," the black troops proved themselves ineffective in combat. He added that "the abolitionists may talk as they please, but I tell you that colored troops cannot be depended on and that evidently caused this great defeat."[19] In his report Major General Ambrose E. Burnside disputed the criticisms of the black troops, explaining, "They certainly moved forward as gallantly under the first fire and until their ranks were broken as any troops I ever saw in action."[20]

Though most observers considered the performance of the USCT at the Crater unsatisfactory, if not disastrous, the battle at New Market Heights, Virginia, on September 29, 1864, erased any doubts about the fighting ability of black troops. The fight at New Market Heights, one of many in Grant's Petersburg-Richmond siege, lasting from June 1864 to March 1865, began before daybreak. It involved more African American troops than any other action of the war. Lieutenant Colonel Giles Shurtleff, commander of the 5th USCT, prepared his men, most of whom came from Ohio, for battle with impossible promises. "If you are brave soldiers," Shurtleff proclaimed, "the stigma of diminished pay must be removed. And the greater stigma of denying you full and equal rights of citizenship shall also be swept away and your race forever rescued from the cruel prejudice and oppression which have been upon you from the foundation of the government."[21]

So inspired, the 5th USCT eagerly joined forces with the 6th, 36th, and 38th USCT regiments under Colonel Alonzo Draper, part of a large force of more than twenty-six thousand Union troops of Major General David B. Birney's 18th Corps arrayed against only a small contingent of eighteen hundred Confederates defending New Market Heights.

The first brigade that Brigadier General Charles J. Paine sent up the steep slopes took severe fire and soon retreated with heavy losses. Paine next dispatched Draper's brigade. Musket fire from the Heights and the obstruction of two abatises (barricades of felled trees with pointed ends facing the enemy) not only slowed Draper's progress but resulted in the death of all commissioned officers from four companies of the 5th USCT. Noncommissioned officers—Sergeants Powhatan Beaty, James H. Bronson, Robert Pinn, and Milton M. Holland—took command of Companies D, G, I, and C. These men, legally barred from commanding troops, nevertheless successfully led their companies in the brigade's routing of the Confederates from the Heights. For their valor each received the Medal of Honor for gallantry. The 5th planted its colors proudly in ground held just minutes before by the Rebels.

The following day, after having given chase to the retreating southerners, the men of the 5th USCT returned to the Heights's Rebel-dug trenches to help repel a Confederate counterattack and held the captured terrain until December. Thomas Morris Chester, an African American journalist who reported on the fight at New Market Heights for the *Philadelphia Press*, heaped praise on the contributions of the black troops. "Let us all be thankful that we have colored troops that will fight, and white officers, and colored ones, too, who can successfully command them to deeds of daring, and may their efforts in this war grow still brighter and brighter," he wrote.[22] As Chester made clear, the African American soldiers had acquitted themselves in combat with dignity and honor. The highly decorated four black sergeants put the lie to many whites' belief that blacks would fight only if led by whites.

Two and a half months later, on December 15, 1864, reveille sounded at 4:00 a.m. in Union camps near Nashville, Tennessee, calling the fifty-five thousand troops under the command of Major General George H. Thomas to rouse themselves and prepare for action. The troops awoke, ate breakfast, and collected their sixty-plus rounds of ammunition, several days worth of rations, blankets, and overcoats. Thomas counted five thousand black troops within his command organized into two brigades. Colonel Thomas Jefferson Morgan led the 1st Colored Brigade, consisting of five regiments. Colonel Charles R. Thompson led the three regiments that composed the 2nd Colored Brigade.

Thomas's battle plan called for Morgan's brigade and another made up of white Ohioans and Indianans, led by Lieutenant Colonel Charles H. Grosvenor, to attack the enemy's rear, catching it by surprise. Once Thompson's brigade heard the guns of the other brigades, it would launch a supporting attack. Battles seldom proceed according to plan, however. Unbeknownst to Morgan, the Rebels, hidden in the trees, watched his men's every step, ruling out any surprise. The sight of black soldiers marching toward them only incensed the waiting Rebels, many of whom had never before faced black troops in battle. Charles Martin of the 1st Georgia Volunteer Regiment recalled that "every step [the African Americans] took . . . was watched by angry eyes and [men] with twitching fingers on gun triggers [who only] awaited the signal to exterminate" the black troops.[23]

What Morgan assumed was a pile of logs before his line of march turned out to be a lunette—a field fortification with a protective ditch in front and four weapons within—guns that soon after opened fire on the bluecoats. Between Morgan and Captain Edward Broughton's Rebels lay a twenty-foot-deep cut in the ground several hundred yards long occupied by the tracks of the Nashville and Chattanooga Railroad. Morgan was unaware of the cut until he stumbled upon it. As Morgan's men approached, "Up rose the line of gray and crash went that deadly volley of lead full into the poor fellows' faces," wrote Private Philip Stephenson, an Arkansan.[24] Another Confederate soldier, Samuel Cook of the 17th Texas Cavalry (dismounted), remembered that once the shooting started they "had a perfect slaughter pen with the Negro soldiers."[25]

Some of Morgan's men jumped for cover into the cut, breaking arms and legs. Broughton's soldiers closed off the mouth of the cut and killed all caught in its opening. Others rushed for cover by leaping into a nearby pond "only to be killed 'until the pond was black.'" "We had the negroes in our trap," exclaimed Martin, "and when we commenced firing on them . . . all that remained on the ground were good niggers"—that is to say, dead ones.[26] Black soldiers who had been spared the slaughter pen immediately rushed into the fray. One trooper stood unprotected in the open, firing and reloading until ordered to take cover. Morgan called a retreat. Having devastated Morgan's troops, the Rebels next turned their fire on Grosvenor's brigade as it entered the fight. With few exceptions, the white troops panicked and streamed toward the rear. Thompson's black brigade skirmished throughout the day with the Confederates farther to the right of where Morgan's troops previously had fought, inflicting and receiving few casualties.

Once again, Morgan's and Thompson's men demonstrated the black soldiers' willingness to fight and die. Morgan lost more than three hundred men. "They fell like wheat before a mowing machine," remembered a Confederate corporal.[27] General Thomas had positioned a line of white soldiers with fixed bayonets some distance behind Morgan's and Thompson's men to bar what

No one looking into the eyes of this soldier, a member of Company B, 103rd USCT, could doubt his determination or, it seems probable, the fighting he had witnessed. Liljenquist Family Collection, Library of Congress.

Thomas feared would be a headlong retreat by the black soldiers once the lead began to fly. But Thomas need not have worried about the blacks' flight.

Following the Nashville campaign Colonel Reuben D. Mussey, then serving as commissioner for the organization of black troops in Middle and East Tennessee, reported on the unflinching service of the USCT that had faced Confederates from the Army of Tennessee under Lieutenant General John Bell Hood. Riding over the battlefield, Mussey found "Black and white dead lay side by side. Death had known no distinction of color, nor had Valor, for the blacks were as near the enemy's line, as were the whites." He identified a number of instances of "conspicuous bravery" by the men of the USCT at Nashville, especially by color-bearers, all of whom were either killed or wounded. In Mussey's opinion, the African Americans proved their merit as soldiers in battle, demonstrating "that the Colored Troops in this department are brave, well disciplined and have good officers, and that henceforth in the army they will have their place beside all other troops. Another proof of the wisdom of our Government, in arming the Blacks has been given." Colonel Henry Stone, who commanded the 100th USCT in the combat, added: "For the first time in the memorable history of the Army of the Cumberland, . . . the blood of white and black men has flowed freely together for the great Cause which is to give freedom, unity, manhood and peace to all men, of whatever birth or complexion."[28]

Black Sailors

Black sailors similarly distinguished themselves in battle. Four won the Navy Medal of Honor. Robert Blake, a powder boy on the U.S.S. *Marblehead* during its Christmas Day 1863 engagement with Confederate ships off Legareville, on South Carolina's Stono River, earned Commander Richard W. Meade Jr.'s high esteem for his actions. He "excited my admiration by the cool and brave manner in which he served," Meade said of Blake.[29] Joachim Pease, a gun loader on the Union gunboat U.S.S. *Kearsarge*, whose guns sunk the Confederate raider C.S.S. *Alabama* on June 19, 1864, off the coast of Cherbourg, France, won his medal for demonstrating extraordinary bravery. John Lawson, a landsman on board the gunboat U.S.S. *Hartford* during the Union navy's capture of Mobile Bay on August 5, 1864, refused treatment after receiving a leg wound and being hurled against the ship's side and "steadfastly continued his duties throughout the remainder of the action."[30] Another landsman, Aaron Anderson, on board the U.S.S. *Wyandank* during its March 17, 1865, mission to rout Confederate boats out of Mattox Creek, a tributary of the Potomac River in Westmoreland County, Virginia, also won the bronze, star-shaped medal. According to his citation, Anderson "carried out his duties courageously in the face of a devastating fire which cut away half the oars, pierced the launch in many places and cut the barrel off a musket being fired at the enemy."[31] Of the 3,220 Union sailors killed, wounded, or missing in action, blacks accounted for about 800. Another two thousand black sailors died of disease.

As the experiences of blacks who served in the U.S. Navy suggest, by the end of the nation's most devastating war African Americans had repeatedly proved their fighting ability and courage. Clearly the USCT performed well in combat, increasingly so after 1864, when properly armed, equipped, and led, they had become "seasoned campaigners."[32] They paid a high price, however. Sixty-eight thousand, or about one man in three, died in uniform from all causes. Of those, 2,751 lost their lives on the battlefield. The rest succumbed to wounds and disease and, in some instances, met death on their way home. Some of the officers of the 11th U.S. Colored Heavy Artillery (originally organized as the 14th Rhode Island Colored Heavy Artillery) who sailed home from New Orleans on the steamer *Atlanta* in the fall 1865 drowned when their ship sank in a storm 250 miles south of Sandy Hook, New Jersey.[33]

Epilogue

By the time General Robert E. Lee surrendered to General Ulysses S. Grant at Appomattox Court House, Virginia, the U.S. Colored Troops had won the respect of many northern whites, citizens and Union soldiers alike, most of whom had originally viewed them with a mixture of skepticism, fear, and disgust. The prominent role of the 22nd USCT at Abraham Lincoln's funeral procession marked a fitting tribute to their accomplishments.

The procession left the White House grounds for the mile-and-a-third trip down Pennsylvania Avenue to the U.S. Capitol at 2:10 p.m. on April 19, 1865, ten minutes behind schedule. There the fallen commander-in-chief's body would lie in state for two days before starting the thirteen-day journey by train back to his home in Springfield, Illinois.

Sixty thousand people, many of them black, most of them hushed, crowded into positions where they could see the entourage. People watched from housetops, trees, and windows. Flags flew at half-mast. Bells tolled. Minute guns, fired in mourning at one minute intervals, delivered salutes. Black crepe hung from buildings and homes.

The procession, which took two hours to pass a given point, consisted of white regiments of the Union army, Lincoln's casket, and a carriage conveying the nation's new president, the Tennessean Andrew Johnson. Lincoln's eldest son, Robert Todd Lincoln, along with senators, cabinet members, gover-

At war's end, after nearly two and a half years of fighting for the Union, the 55th Massachusetts Volunteer Regiment marched through the streets of Charleston, South Carolina. *Harper's Weekly*, March 18, 1865.

nors, congressmen and other officials followed. Secretary of the Navy Gideon Welles noted "the poor colored people who crowded the streets, joined the procession, and exhibited their woe, bewailing the loss of him whom they regarded as a benefactor and father."[1] Thousands of people, black and white, took up positions at the end of the procession.

Leading the procession as it neared the Capitol came the 22nd USCT led by Colonel Joseph B. Kiddoo, a battle-tested Pennsylvania veteran who had taken command of the 22nd in May 1864. Secretary of War Stanton had asked Major General Godfrey Weitzel, the German-born commander of all Union troops north of Appomattox, to select a black regiment to march in the procession. Weitzel chose the 22nd because of its reputation for exceptional discipline and soldiering. Kiddoo's regiment waited for the procession in front of the Metropolitan Hotel at Sixth Street and Pennsylvania Avenue NW.

As the procession neared the hotel, a band struck up a dirge, and the soldiers marched to the front in dress uniforms with white gloves and fixed bayonets. They marched with muskets reversed, following funerary regulation, their eyes focused straight ahead, looking neither right nor left. "Their admirable marching and soldierly bearing was remarked by all, and formed one of the most prominent features of the occasion," wrote a reporter for the *Chicago Tribune*.[2] Following the funeral, Stanton dispatched the 22nd to Chapel Point in southern Maryland to help search for Lincoln's assassin, the noted actor and southern sympathizer John Wilkes Booth.

Many white southerners shared Booth's hatred of Lincoln and retained their disunionist sentiments. Andrew Johnson was himself a former slaveholder who favored a generous peace for the South and hoped to readmit the former Confederate states to the Union with few conditions beyond emancipation. Yet the vast majority of white southerners refused to relinquish their region's culture of white supremacy. As a result, during early Presidential Reconstruction southern legislators enacted "Black Codes," conferring upon the freedpeople certain limited rights, including the right to marry (but only to another black), to sign contracts, to acquire property, and to testify in court (but only in cases involving blacks). In many cases the codes also forced blacks to sign yearly labor contracts if they wanted to work. Those who did not sign such agreements could be arrested, fined, and, if unable to pay, forced to work for an employer who would pay the fine. Children of indigent freed parents could be apprenticed to whites. Blacks could neither vote nor serve on police forces or in state militias. Deep-seated prejudice generally prevented blacks from receiving fair trials. Freedmen and freedwomen found themselves in conditions not far removed from slavery and especially vulnerable to all manner of racial violence.

The Black Codes and similar repressive measures passed by the former Confederate state legislatures undermined public support in the North and in Congress for Johnson's laissez-faire Reconstruction program. In response, between 1865 and 1870 Congress passed three far-reaching amendments to the Constitution to protect the fruits of emancipation. The Thirteenth Amendment (ratified December 6, 1865) banned slavery. The Fourteenth Amendment (ratified July 9, 1868) defined U.S. citizenship and enacted critical protections for all U.S. citizens at both the state and federal levels. The Fifteenth Amendment (ratified February 3, 1870) extended voting rights to African American males of age. Congress acted again in 1875 when it passed the Civil Rights Act of that year. This measure guaranteed all citizens, black

Joining the Union army meant leaving family behind for long periods of time. Here an unidentified soldier on leave—likely from one of the seven USCT regiments raised in Maryland—poses in full uniform with his wife and two daughters. Liljenquist Family Collection, Library of Congress.

and white, equal access to public accommodations, including inns, hotels, trains, steamboats, and theaters.

Despite its good intentions, Congress provided few penalties for individuals or states that violated the new federal laws. Blacks subjected to racial violence, including murder, were left to the mercy of state and local governments. In 1883 the U.S. Supreme Court declared the 1875 Civil Rights Act unconstitutional. Increasingly cities, counties, and states, most notably in the South, enacted laws that banished blacks from public accommodations and prevented them from voting through outright violence but also through such proscriptive devices as grandfather clauses, literacy tests, and poll taxes. As a result the freedpeople rarely received legal protection or redress. During the 1870s former Confederates regained control of the southern state governments and systematically passed rigid segregation laws—the so-called Jim Crow laws. De jure segregation quickly became the norm in southern race relations and lasted into the 1960s. De facto segregation continues well into the twenty-first century.

In terms of civil rights, following the Civil War USCT soldiers fared no better than did the black citizenry at large. While, significantly, the Army Reorganization Act in 1866 for the first time excluded any reference to race, military examiners nonetheless rejected the application of every black Civil War veteran for a commission in the regular army. Sergeant Major Christian A. Fleetwood of the 4th USCT, who received a Medal of Honor for his valor at the Battle of Chaffin's Farm, failed to receive a commission even after every officer in his regiment recommended to Secretary of War Stanton that he receive one. Disgusted by such injustice, Fleetwood remarked, "I see no good that will result to our people by continuing to serve" in the army. "On the contrary," he added, "it seems to me that our continuing to Act in a subordinate capacity, with no hope of advancement or promotion is an absolute injury to our cause. It is a tacit but telling acknowledgement on our part that we are not fit for promotion, & that we are satisfied to remain in a state of marked and acknowledged subserviency."[3] Fleetwood continued to serve in the army until honorably discharged in May 1866.

Blacks who did serve in the post–Civil War army did so in one of four black units: two cavalry troops (the 9th and 10th) and two infantry regiments (the 24th and 25th). Many of these so-called Buffalo Soldiers, including the pioneer African American historian George Washington Williams, had prior military experience. Williams, who joined the 10th Cavalry following the war, had served in the 41st USCT. With but rare exception, however, whites filled the commissioned officer ranks in America's post–Civil War segregated army.

Blacks made minor advances as officers during the Spanish-American War. During that conflict several African American regiments had black lieutenants. Officers of color served in state militia units recruited in Illinois, Kansas, and North Carolina. During World War I the army established at Fort Des Moines, Iowa, its first officer training program for blacks since Webster's 1863 Free Military School for Applicants for Commands of Colored Troops. The men graduated as captains and lieutenants served in black regiments, which, for the most part, performed fatigue duty in Europe. World War II witnessed more blacks, officers and enlisted men, assigned to combat duty, though they remained in segregated units. And the majority of black GIs continued to perform fatigue work. Following the war, on July 26, 1948, President Harry S. Truman issued Executive Order 9981, which called for equality of opportunity in all branches of the armed forces. By the end of the Korean War in 1953, Truman's order largely had integrated the armed forces. The United States no longer had the distinction, many would say the moral opprobrium, of having a Jim Crow army.

In the post–World War II decades fulfillment of the promises of equality in return for military service inched along ever so slowly. The U.S. Supreme Court's 1954 *Brown v. Board of Education* decision signaled the beginning of the end of decades-long segregation in the nation's public schools. Not until the mid-1960s, however, a century after Appomattox, did black citizens gain the protection of the landmark civil rights legislation of President Lyndon B. Johnson's "Great Society." True across-the-board equality, however, would continue to prove elusive for the remainder of the twentieth century and into the new millennium. The struggles of the U.S. Colored Troops remained distant reminders of opportunities won and lost—the legacy of slavery, white racism, and military service in the land of the free.

NOTES

PROLOGUE

1. Gillmore and Seymour quoted in Bernard C. Nalty, *Strength for the Fight: A History of Black Americans in the Military* (New York: Free Press, 1986), 38.

2. Luis F. Emilio, *A Brave Black Regiment: History of the Fifty-Fourth Regiment of Massachusetts Volunteer Infantry, 1863–1865* (1894; reprint, Salem, NH: Ayer, 1990), 92.

3. Wickliffe and Mallory quoted in John David Smith, "Let Us All Be Grateful That We Have Colored Troops That Will Fight," in *Black Soldiers in Blue: African American Troops in the Civil War Era*, ed. Smith (Chapel Hill: University of North Carolina Press, 2002), 10–11.

CHAPTER ONE: How Racism Impeded the Recruitment of Black Soldiers

1. Bernard C. Nalty, *Strength for the Fight: A History of Black Americans in the Military* (New York: Free Press, 1986), 18.

2. Wilson quoted in Benjamin Quarles, *The Negro in the Civil War* (1953; reprint, Boston: Little, Brown, 1969), 24.

3. Green quoted in J. Matthew Gallman, *Mastering Wartime: A Social History of Philadelphia during the Civil War* (1990; reprint, Philadelphia: University of Pennsylvania Press, 2000), 45.

4. John David Hoptak, "A Forgotten Hero of the Civil War," *Pennsylvania Heritage* 36 (Spring 2010): 6–13.

5. John M. Langston, *From the Virginia Plantation to the National Capitol* (1894; reprint, New York: Arno, 1969), 206, quoted in Versalle F. Washington, *Eagles on Their Buttons: A Black Infantry Regiment in the Civil War* (Columbia: University of Missouri Press, 1999), 2–3.

6. Governor William A. Buckingham, in *Norwich Bulletin*, Aug. 27, 1861, quoted in Diana Ross McCain, *Connecticut African American Soldiers in the Civil War, 1861–1865* (Hartford: Connecticut Historical Committee, 2000), 10.

7. Brannigan quoted in Quarles, *The Negro in the Civil War*, 31.

8. "The Enlistment of Negro Soldiers," *Brooklyn Daily Eagle*, July 31, 1863, p. 2.

9. Alexander H. Stephens, "Sketch of the Cornerstone Speech," in Henry Cleveland, *Alexander H. Stephens, in Public and Private: With Letters and Speeches, before, during, and since the War* (Philadelphia: National, 1886), 722.

10. George H. Hepworth, *The Whip, Hoe, and Sword; or, The Gulf-Department in '63*, ed. Joe Gray Taylor (1864; reprint, Baton Rouge: Louisiana State University Press, 1979), 187.

11. Mary Boykin Miller Chesnut, *Mary Chesnut's Civil War*, ed. C. Vann Woodward (New Haven, CT: Yale University Press, 1981), 36.

12. Henrietta Buckmaster, *Let My People Go: The Story of the Underground Railroad and the Growth of the Abolition Movement* (New York: Harper and Brothers, 1941), 296.

13. Maury quoted in Charles H. Wesley and Patricia W. Romero, *Negro Americans in the Civil War: From Slavery to Citizenship* (New York: Publishers Co., 1967), 58.

14. James Montgomery to Mrs. George Stearns, Apr. 25, 1863, quoted in Dudley Taylor Cornish, *The Sable Arm: Negro Troops in the Union Army, 1861–1865* (New York: Longmans, Green, 1956), 182.

15. Untitled *New York Times* article, reprinted in *National Intelligencer*, May 27, 1862, quoted in Cornish, *The Sable Arm*, 40.

16. Untitled *Boston Journal* article, reprinted in *National Intelligencer*, May 30, 1862, quoted in Cornish, *The Sable Arm*, 41.

17. Benjamin Butler to Mrs. Butler, Aug. 2, 1862, in Benjamin F. Butler, *Private and Official Correspondence of Gen. Benjamin F. Butler during the Period of the Civil War*, 5 vols. (Norwood, MA: Plimpton, 1917), 2:148, quoted in Cornish, *The Sable Arm*, 62.

18. Stanton to Lane, Sept. 23, 1862, in *The War of the Rebellion: A Compilation of the Official Records of the Union and Confederate Armies*, 128 vols. (Washington, DC: Government Printing Office, 1880–1901) (hereafter *OR*), ser. 3, vol. 1, part 3, p. 582, quoted in Cornish, *The Sable Arm*, 75.

19. James Lane in *Leavenworth Daily Conservative*, Aug. 6, 1862, quoted in Cornish, *The Sable Arm*, 75.

20. "Kansas Correspondence: The Kansas Colored Regiment," *Chicago Tribune*, Nov. 7, 1862, p. 2.

21. Esther Hill Hawks, *A Woman Doctor's Civil War: Esther Hill Hawks' Diary*, ed. Gerald Schwartz (Columbia: University of South Carolina Press, 1984), 46.

22. Saxton to Higginson, Nov. 5, 1862, in Thomas Wentworth Higginson, *Army Life in a Black Regiment* (1870; reprint, Mineola, NY: Dover, 2002), 2.

23. Camp Diary, January 7, [1863], in Higginson, *Army Life*, 28.

24. Higginson, *Army Life*, 110.

25. G. M. Wells to E. L. Pierce, undated, in *OR*, ser. 3, vol. 2, pp. 58–59.

26. Higginson, *Army Life*, 38.

27. W. P. Derby, *Twenty-Seventh Massachusetts Regiment Volunteer Infantry during the Civil War, 1861–1865* (Boston: Wright and Potter, 1883), 192, quoted in Richard M. Reid, *Freedom for Themselves: North Carolina's Black Soldiers in the Civil War* (Chapel Hill: University of North Carolina Press, 2008), 32.

28. "The Employment of Negroes as Soldiers," *New York Times*, Aug. 6, 1862, p. 5.

29. Abraham Lincoln, *The Collected Works of Abraham Lincoln*, ed. Roy P. Basler, 8 vols. (New Brunswick, NJ: Rutgers University Press, 1953), 5:423, quoted in James M. McPherson, *The Negro's Civil War: How American Blacks Felt and Acted during the War for the Union* (1965; reprint, New York: Vintage Books, 1993), 164.

30. Lincoln to A. G. Hodges, Esq., Apr. 4, 1864, in *The Collected Works of Abraham Lincoln*, 7:281–82.

CHAPTER TWO: How Slaves and Freedmen Earned Their Brass Buttons

1. "The Colored Regiment," *Chicago Tribune*, Jan. 18, 1864, p. 4.

2. The Negro in the Military Service of the United States, 1639–1886, file M858, roll 2, p. 1163, National Archives and Records Administration, Washington, DC (hereafter NARA).

3. J. W. M. Appleton, "A Glorious Campaign: The Journal of Major J. W. M. Appleton, 54th Massachusetts Infantry," ed. John A. Cuthbert (unpublished manuscript, November 2007, West Virginia University Libraries, Morgantown), 22.

4. Norwood P. Hallowell, *The Negro as a Soldier in the War of the Rebellion* (1897), quoted in John David Smith, "Let Us All Be Grateful That We Have Colored Troops That Will Fight," in *Black Soldiers in Blue: African American Troops in the Civil War Era*, ed. Smith (Chapel Hill: University of North Carolina Press, 2002), 29.

5. Shaw to Annie, Feb. 4, 1863, in *Blue-Eyed Child of Fortune: The Civil War Letters of Colonel Robert Gould Shaw*, ed. Russell Duncan (Athens: University of Georgia Press, 1992), 283.

6. Shaw to Mother, Mar. 25, 1863, in ibid., 313.

7. The Negro in the Military Service of the United States, roll 2, p. 1160.

8. Ibid., 1222.

9. Shaw, *Blue-Eyed Child*, xiii.

10. Appleton, "A Glorious Campaign," 22.

11. *Boston Pilot* quoted in Shaw, *Blue-Eyed Child*, 40.

12. "Speech of Frederick Douglass," *Liberator*, July 24, 1863, p. 118.

13. Bussey to Curtis, Jan. 13, 1863, The Negro in the Military Service of the United States, 3 (2), Record Group 94, Records of the Adjutant Generals Office, 1780s–1917, NARA, quoted in Michael T. Meier, "Lorenzo Thomas and the Recruitment of Blacks in the Mississippi Valley, 1863–1865," in Smith, *Black Soldiers in Blue*, 251.

14. H. W. Halleck to Maj. Gen'l U.S. Grant, Mar. 31, 1863, quoted in George Washington Williams, *A History of Negro Troops in the War of the Rebellion, 1861–1865* (New York: Harper and Brothers, 1887), 107.

15. "Adjt. Gen. Thomas' Advice to the Negroes; His Speech to the Contrabands at Memphis," *New York Times*, June 7, 1863, p. 6.

16. Thomas quoted in "The Negro Troops in the Southwest," *Harper's Weekly*, Nov. 14, 1863, p. 721, quoted in Meier, "Lorenzo Thomas," 257–58.

17. Lorenzo Thomas, Orders and Letters, in Generals' Papers and Books, 140

vols., unnumbered, War Records Division, p. 10, NARA, quoted in Dudley Taylor Cornish, *The Sable Arm: Negro Troops in the Union Army, 1861–1865* (New York: Longmans, Green, 1956), 117, 118.

18. Report of the Committee on the Judiciary on the Case of William Yokum, June 20, 1864, H.R. Rep. No. 118 (1864), 2:1–4.

19. Lincoln to Glenn, Feb. 7, 1865, to Edwin M. Stanton, Feb. [7?], 1865, in *Collected Works of Abraham Lincoln*, ed. Roy P. Basler, 8 vols. (New Brunswick, NJ: Rutgers University Press, 1953), 8:266, 268.

20. Sherman to William M. McPherson, [ca. Sept. 15–30, 1864], in *Sherman's Civil War: Selected Correspondence of William T. Sherman, 1860–1865*, ed. Brooks D. Simpson and Jean V. Berlin (Chapel Hill: University of North Carolina Press, 1999), 727.

21. David M. Gold, "Frustrated Glory: John Francis Appleton and Black Soldiers in the Civil War," *Maine Historical Society Quarterly* 31 (Summer 1991): 203n34.

22. Thomas Wentworth Higginson, *Army Life in a Black Regiment* (1870; reprint, Mineola, NY: Dover Publications, 2002), 173.

23. John Van Horne, ed., *Phil Lapsansky: Appreciations, A Collection of Essays Honoring Phillip S. Lapsansky on His Retirement after More than Forty Years of Service to the Library Company of Philadelphia, 1971–2012* (Philadelphia: Library Company of Philadelphia, 2012), 101.

24. "Enlistment of Colored Regiments," *Liberator*, July 17, 1863, p. 114.

25. "Enthusiasm among the Colored People," *Liberator*, July 3, 1863, p. 107.

26. "The Fifth Ohio Colored Regiment," *Cincinnati Daily Gazette*, Nov. 12, 1863, p. 1.

27. Statements by John W. Bantum in "Murder of Lieut. Eben White," June 19, 1874, H.R. Exec. Doc. No. 281, 43rd Cong., 1st sess. (Washington, DC: Government Printing Office, 1874), 1–8.

28. Cope to Bramlette, July 8, 1864, Bramlette Papers, box 5, folder 99, Filson Historical Society Special Collections, Louisville, KY, quoted in Meier, "Lorenzo Thomas," 266.

29. *Lowell (MA) Daily Citizen and News*, Oct. 21, 1863, p. 1.

30. Bramlette to Lincoln, Sept. 3, 1864, quoted in Meier, "Lorenzo Thomas," 267.

31. Johnson to Stanton, Sept. 11, 1863, *The War of the Rebellion: A Compilation of the Official Records of the Union and Confederate Armies*, 128 vols. (Washington, DC: Government Printing Office, 1880–1901) (hereafter *OR*), ser. 3, vol. 3, pp. 819–20.

32. Stanton to Stearns, Sept. 18, 1863, in ibid., 823.

33. John Hope Franklin, "James T. Ayers, Civil War Recruiter," *Journal of the Illinois State Historical Society* 40 (Sept. 1947): 278–79.

34. *The Diary of James T. Ayers Civil War Recruiter*, ed. John Hope Franklin (Springfield: Illinois State Historical Society, 1947), 40, 32–33.

35. Ibid., 46, 47, 49, 54.

36. Sullivan quoted in James M. McPherson, *Marching toward Freedom: Blacks in the Civil War, 1861–1865* (New York: Alfred A. Knopf, 1967), 62.

37. Keith P. Wilson, *Campfires of Freedom: The Camp Life of Black Soldiers during the Civil War* (Kent, OH: Kent State University Press, 2002), 224.

38. Kennedy to Hon. E. M. Stanton, July 8, 1863, *OR*, ser. 3, vol. 3, p. 473.

39. Stanton to Governor Andrew, July 8, 1863, in ibid., 473–74.

40. *New York Times*, Mar. 7, 1864, quoted in Cornish, *The Sable Arm*, 254.

CHAPTER THREE: How White Officers Learned to Command Black Troops

1. "Our Baton Rouge Correspondence," *New York Herald*, Feb. 4, 1863, p. 2.

2. "The Negro Troops," *New York Times*, Feb. 21, 1863, p. 4.

3. *Free Military School for Applicants for Commands of Colored Troops, no. 1210 Chestnut Street, Philadelphia: Established by the Supervisory Committee for Recruiting Colored Regiments, Chief Preceptor, John H. Taggart, Late Colonel 12th Regiment Pennsylvania Reserves* (Philadelphia: King and Baird, 1864).

4. Andrew to Francis Shaw, Jan. 30, 1863, in Luis F. Emilio, *A Brave Black Regiment: History of the 54th Regiment of Massachusetts Volunteer Infantry 1863–1865* (1894), quoted in Joseph T. Glatthaar, *Forged in Battle: The Civil War Alliance of Black Soldiers and White Officers* (New York: Free Press, 1990), 37.

5. Lorenzo Thomas to Gen. John A. McClernand, Orders and Letters of Brigadier General Lorenzo Thomas, Generals' Papers and Books, 140 vols., unnumbered, 52, War Records Division, National Archives and Records Administration, Washington, DC (hereafter NARA), quoted in Dudley Taylor Cornish, *The Sable Arm: Negro Troops in the Union Army, 1861–1865* (New York: Longmans, Green, 1956), 206.

6. J. W. M. Appleton, "A Glorious Campaign: The Journal of Major J. W. M. Appleton, 54th Massachusetts Infantry," ed. John A. Cuthbert (unpublished manuscript, November 2007, West Virginia University Libraries, Morgantown), 10.

7. Henry to Parents & all, Nov. 28, 1863, Henry Crydenwise Papers, Emory University, quoted in Glatthaar, *Forged in Battle*, 40.

8. Ibid., 41.

9. Illinois soldier in Freeman S. Bowley, *A Boy Lieutenant* (Philadelphia: H. Altemus, 1906), quoted in Glatthaar, *Forged in Battle*, 41.

10. Oliver W. Norton to Sister L., Oct. 15, 1863, in Norton, *Army Letters* (Chicago: O. L. Deming, 1903), quoted in Glatthaar, *Forged in Battle*, 41.

11. Milroy to Stanton, Feb. 2, 1865, Abraham Lincoln Papers, ser. 1, General Correspondence, Manuscript Division, Library of Congress, Washington, DC.

12. Mussey to Col. R. W. Barnard, Maj. Wm Inness, & Maj. E. Grosskopff, Nov. 3, 1864, Record Group 393, NARA, quoted in Glatthaar, *Forged in Battle*, 48.

13. Cornish, *The Sable Arm*, 224–25.

14. Samuel Evans to Father, in Robert F. Engs and Corey M. Brooks, eds., *Their Patriotic Duty: The Civil War Letters of the Evans Family of Brown County, Ohio* (New York: Fordham University Press, 2007), 155–56, quoted in Glenn Robins, *They Have Left Us Here to Die: The Civil War Prison Diary of Sgt. Lyle Adair, 111th U.S. Colored Infantry* (Kent, OH: Kent State University Press, 2011), 9.

15. John McMurray, *Recollections of a Colored Troop* (1916; reprint, Brookville, PA: McMurray, 1994), 1–2.

16. *Proceedings of General Court Martial Trial of Maj. W. S. Long*, LL 2999, Record Group 153, NARA, quoted in Glatthaar, *Forged in Battle*, 52.

17. Dan'l to Brother, Feb. 26, 1864, Densmore Family Papers, Minnesota Historical Society, Saint Paul, Minnesota, quoted in Glatthaar, *Forged in Battle*, 52.

18. Lloyd to General Lorenzo Thomas, Apr. 11, 1864, Record Group 94, 1863 I–Z, 1864 A–L, box 3, NARA.

19. Laird to General Lorenzo Thomas, July 13, 1864, Record Group 94, 1863 I–Z, 1864 A–L, box 3, NARA.

20. R. K. Beecham, *As If It Were Glory: Robert Beecham's Civil War from the Iron Brigade to the Black Regiments*, ed. Michael E. Stevens (Madison, WI: Madison House, 1998), 152, 159.

21. Casey to Webster, Mar. 7, 1864, in *Free Military School for Applicants for Commands of Colored Troops* (1863), quoted in Keith Wilson, "Thomas Webster and the Free Military School for Applicants for Commands of Colored Troops," *Civil War History* 29 (June 1983): 103.

22. *Free Military School Prospectus* (1863), quoted in Wilson, "Thomas Webster and the Free Military School," 106.

23. Testimony in *The War of the Rebellion: A Compilation of the Official Records of the Union and Confederate Armies*, 128 vols. (Washington, DC: Government Printing Office, 1880–1901) (hereafter *OR*), ser. 1, vol. 26, part 1, p. 468, quoted in Fred Harvey Harrington, "The Fort Jackson Mutiny," *Journal of Negro History* 27 (Oct. 1942): 422.

24. Testimony in *OR*, ser. 1, vol. 26, part 1, p. 460, quoted in Harrington, "The Fort Jackson Mutiny," 423.

25. William A. Dobak, *Freedom by the Sword: The U.S. Colored Troops, 1862–1867* (Washington, DC: U.S. Army Center of Military History, 2011), 116.

26. Sam Evans to Sister, Oct. 13, 1863, Peet Family Papers, Minnesota Historical Society, Saint Paul, Minnesota, quoted in Glatthaar, *Forged in Battle*, 56.

27. Andrew Evans to Son, May 18, 1863, Evans Family Papers, Ohio Historical Society, Columbus, OH, quoted in Glatthaar, *Forged in Battle*, 56–57.

28. Henry to Parents & all, Nov. 28, 1863, quoted in Glatthaar, *Forged in Battle*, 56.

29. O. Densmore to Son, Jan. 1, 1865, Densmore Family Papers, quoted in Glatthaar, *Forged in Battle*, 56.

30. Benjamin F. Butler, *Private and Official Correspondence of Gen. Benjamin F. Butler during the Period of the Civil War*, 5 vols. (Norwood, MA: Plimpton, 1917), quoted in Benjamin Quarles, *The Negro in the Civil War* (1953; reprint, Boston: Little, Brown, 1969), 116–17.

31. *New Bedford Mercury*, Jan. 28, 1864, quoted in Noah Andre Trudeau, *Like Men of War: Black Troops in the Civil War, 1862–1865* (Boston: Little, Brown, 1998), 373.

32. Edward W. Kinsley Papers, Duke University, quoted in Trudeau, *Like Men of War*, 374.

33. Appleton, "A Glorious Campaign," 216.

34. Christian G. Samito, *Becoming American under Fire: Irish Americans, African Americans, and the Politics of Citizenship during the Civil War Era* (Ithaca, NY: Cornell University Press, 2009), 63.

CHAPTER FOUR: How Blacks Became Soldiers

1. Robert Cowden, *A Brief Sketch of the Organization and Services of the Fifty-Ninth Regiment of the United States Colored Infantry and Biographical Sketches* (Dayton, OH: United Brethren, 1883), 45–46.

2. Thomas Wentworth Higginson, *The Complete Civil War Journal and Selected Letters of Thomas Wentworth Higginson*, ed. Christopher Looby (Chicago: University of Chicago Press, 2000), 99, 320.

3. Brig. Gen. Birney to Maj. C. W. Foster, June 2, 1864, W-190, 1863 Letters Received, ser. 360, Colored Troops Division, Record Group 94, National Archives and Records Administration, Washington, DC (hereafter NARA), quoted in Keith P. Wilson, *Campfires of Freedom: The Camp Life of Black Soldiers during the Civil War* (Kent, OH: Kent State University Press, 2002), 63.

4. J. Garrard to R. S. Davis, Apr. 9, 1864, Regimental Books, 1st U.S. Colored Calvary: Regimental Letters Sent, vol. 1, no. 4, p. 21, Record Group 94, NARA, quoted in Noah Andre Trudeau, "Proven Themselves in Every Respect to Be Men: Black Cavalry in the Civil War," in *Black Soldiers in Blue: African American Troops in the Civil War Era*, ed. John David Smith (Chapel Hill: University of North Carolina Press, 2002), 286; Thomas quoted in Benjamin Quarles, *The Negro in the Civil War* (1953; reprint, Boston: Little, Brown, 1969), 204–5.

5. William A. Dobak, *Freedom by the Sword: The U.S. Colored Troops, 1862–1867* (Washington, DC: U.S. Army Center of Military History, 2011), 20–21.

6. Edward M. Main, *The Story of the Marches, Battles, and Incidents of the Third United States Colored Cavalry: A Fighting Regiment in the War of the Rebellion, 1861–5* (Louisville, KY: Globe, 1908), 58, quoted in Trudeau, "Proven Themselves in Every Respect to Be Men," 285.

7. *The War of the Rebellion: A Compilation of the Official Records of the Union and Confederate Armies*, 128 vols. (Washington, DC: Government Printing Office, 1880–1901) (hereafter *OR*), ser. 1, vol. 39, part 3, p. 476, quoted in Trudeau, "Proven Themselves in Every Respect to Be Men," 286.

8. Thomas J. Morgan, *Reminiscences of Service with the Colored Troops in the Army of the Cumberland* (Providence: Soldiers and Sailors Historical Society of Rhode Island, 1885), 12–13.

9. Ibid., 13.

10. Benjamin Thompson, "Back to the South: The Benjamin Thompson Memoir, Part II," *Civil War Times Illustrated* 12 (Nov. 1973): 28–29.

11. J. J. Holloway to "Dear Friend," Mar. 7, 1864, Exec. Dept. Letters, Letters Received, vol. 59, nos. 50, 148, Andrew Papers, Commonwealth of Massachusetts State Archives, Boston, quoted in Wilson, *Campfires of Freedom*, 31.

12. Wilbur Nelson Diary, June 23, 1864, Nelson Family Papers, Michigan State University; David Cornwell's memoir, "Dan Caverno," p. 129, U.S. Army Military History Institute, Civil War Miscellaneous Collection; B. Marshall Mills to Father, Apr. 11, 1864, Caleb Mills Papers, Indiana Historical Society. Also see William to James, May 11, 1863, William Parkinson Papers, Emory University, in Joseph T. Glatthaar, *Forged in Battle: The Civil War Alliance of Black Soldiers and White Officers* (New York: Free Press, 1990), 102.

13. Thomas Montgomery to Parents and Brothers, Mar. 8, 1864, Montgomery Papers, Minnesota Historical Society, Saint Paul, quoted in Glatthaar, *Forged in Battle*, 101.

14. Proceedings of General Court Martial, Trial of William Walker, MM 1320, Record Group 153, NARA, quoted in Glatthaar, *Forged in Battle*, 112.

15. Ibid., 116.

16. Price Warefield et al. to Stanton, Feb. 20, 1865, in Ira Berlin, ed., *Freedom: A Documentary History of Emancipation, 1861–1867*, ser. 2, *The Black Military Experience* (Cambridge: Cambridge University Press, 1982), quoted in Glatthaar, *Forged in Battle*, 116.

17. *U.S. Infantry Tactics, for the Instruction, Exercise, and Manoeuvres, of the Soldier, a Company, Line of Skirmishers, and Battalion; for the Use of the Colored Troops of the United States Infantry* (New York: Van Nostrand, 1863), 24–25.

18. "The Negro Troops in the Federal Service," *Manchester Guardian*, Feb. 7, 1865, p. 5.

19. Quoted in "The War on the Mississippi: The Negro Regiments," *New York Times*, May 31, 1863, p. 3.

20. Quoted in Heather Andrea Williams, "'Commenced to Think Like a Man': Literacy and Manhood in African American Civil War Regiments," in *Southern Manhood: Perspectives on Masculinity in the Old South*, ed. Craig Thompson Friend and Lorri Glover (Athens: University of Georgia Press, 2004), 205.

21. J. R. Bowles to General Lorenzo Thomas, Sept. 1, Oct. 1, 1864, in Noah Andre Trudeau, ed., *Voices of the 55th: Letters from the 55th Massachusetts Volunteers, 1861–1865* (Dayton, OH: Morningside House, 1996), 227, 228–29.

22. Susie King Taylor, *Reminiscences of My Life in Camp* (1902; reprint, New York: Arno, 1968), 5, 21.

23. Chaplain E. S. Wheeler to Brig. Gen. D. Ullmann, Apr. 8, 1864, D. Ullmann Letters and Orders, Generals' Papers and Books, ser. 159, Record Group 94, NARA, quoted in Wilson, *Campfires of Freedom*, 101–2.

24. T. S. Johnson, Chaplaincy Reports, Feb. 28, Mar. 31, 1865, Thomas S. Johnson Papers, State Historical Society of Wisconsin, Madison, quoted in Wilson, *Campfires of Freedom*, 102.

25. Chaplain G. L. Barnes to Brig. Gen. L. Thomas, Mar. 31, 1865, B-726, 1865, Letters Received, ser. 12, Record Group 94, NARA, quoted in Wilson, *Campfires of Freedom*, 106.

26. "Official Order of the Governor," Mar. 23, 1863, Issuances, 54th Mass. Vols.,

Regimental Books and Papers, U.S. Vol. Org., Record Group 94, NARA, quoted in Wilson, *Campfires of Freedom*, 111.

27. *Christian Recorder*, Dec. 24, 31, 1864, quoted in Wilson, *Campfires of Freedom*, 115.

28. *Christian Recorder*, July 8, 1864, quoted in Wilson, *Campfires of Freedom*, 118.

29. Wilson, *Campfires of Freedom*, 69–70.

30. "Negro Troops," *New York Times*, Feb. 21, 1863, p. 4.

31. Berlin, *Freedom: A Documentary History*, ser. 2, 484–85, 501; Freeman quoted in Susan-Mary Grant, "Fighting for Freedom: African-American Soldiers in the Civil War," in *The American Civil War: Explorations and Reconsiderations*, ed. Susan-Mary Grant and Brian Holden Reid (Harlow, UK: Pearson Education Limited, 2000), 205.

32. Lorenzo Thomas to E. M. Stanton, Nov. 7, 1864, in *OR*, ser. 3, vol. 4, pp. 921–22.

33. Wilson, *Campfires of Freedom*, 13–14, 80.

34. Ibid., 161–62.

CHAPTER FIVE: How Black Troops Gained the Glory and Paid the Price

1. John Cimprich and Robert C. Mainfort Jr., eds., "Fort Pillow Revisited: New Evidence About an Old Controversy," *Civil War History* 28 (Dec. 1982): 294, quoted in John Cimprich, "The Fort Pillow Massacre: Assessing the Evidence," in *Black Soldiers in Blue: African American Troops in the Civil War Era*, ed. John David Smith (Chapel Hill: University of North Carolina Press, 2002), 158.

2. "The Fort Pillow Massacre," *New York Daily Tribune*, Apr. 27, 1864, p. 1.

3. Theodore Hodgkins to E. M. Stanton, Apr. 18, 1864, in Ira Berlin, ed., *Freedom: A Documentary History of Emancipation, 1861–1867*, ser. 2, *The Black Military Experience* (Cambridge: Cambridge University Press, 1982), 587.

4. Mamie Yeary, comp., *Reminiscences of the Boys in Grey, 1861–1865* (Dallas: Smith and Lamar, 1912), 347, quoted in Anne J. Bailey and Daniel E. Sutherland, eds., *Civil War Arkansas: Beyond Battles and Leaders* (Fayetteville: University of Arkansas Press, 2000), 227.

5. "Negro Soldiers Engaged," *Philadelphia Inquirer*, May 26, 1864, p. 1.

6. [Gus] to wife, June 21, 1864, Charles Augustus Hill Papers, Richard S. Tracy Private Collection, quoted in Joseph T. Glatthaar, *Forged in Battle: The Civil War Alliance of Black Soldiers and White Officers* (New York: Free Press, 1990), 149–50.

7. Holcomb in Henry Martyn Cross, "A Yankee Soldier Looks at the Negro," ed. William Cullen Bryant II, *Civil War History* 7 (June 1961): 144, quoted in Randall C. Jimerson, *The Private Civil War: Popular Thought through the Sectional Conflict* (Baton Rouge: Louisiana State University Press, 1988), 97.

8. Banks to Halleck, May 30, 1863, in *The War of the Rebellion: A Compilation of the Official Records of the Union and Confederate Armies*, 128 vols. (Washington, DC: Government Printing Office, 1880–1901) (hereafter *OR*), ser. 1, vol. 26, part 1, p. 45, quoted in Glatthaar, *Forged in Battle*, 129.

9. "Negro Soldiers—the Question Settled and Its Consequences," *New York Times*, June 11, 1863, p. 4.

10. Ullmann to Stanton, June 6, 1863, The Negro in the Military Service of the United States, 1639–1886, file M-858, roll 2, p. 1298, National Archives and Records Administration, Washington, DC.

11. Cyrus Sears, *Paper of Cyrus Sears, Read Before the Ohio Commandery of the Loyal Legion, October 7, 1908* (Columbus, OH: F. J. Heer, 1909), 12, quoted in Richard Lowe, "Battle on the Levee: The Fight at Milliken's Bend," in Smith, *Black Soldiers in Blue*, 110.

12. David D. Porter to Grant, June 7, 1863, *OR*, ser. 1, vol. 24, part 2, p. 454, quoted in Glatthaar, *Forged in Battle*, 134.

13. Elias S. Dennis to Colonel, June 12, 1863, quoted in Ira Berlin, Joseph P. Reidy, and Leslie S. Rowland, eds., *Freedom's Soldiers: The Black Military Experience in the Civil War* (Cambridge: Cambridge University Press, 1998), 98–99.

14. Oliver Willcox Norton to father, March 1, 1863, in *Army Letters, 1861–1865* (Chicago: privately published by the author, 1903), 202.

15. Hamilton in *OR*, ser. 1, vol. 35, part 1, p. 312, quoted in Arthur W. Bergeron Jr., "The Battle of Olustee," in Smith, *Black Soldiers in Blue*, 146.

16. Lawrence Jackson, "As I Saw and Remember the Battle of Olustee, Which Was Fought February 20, 1864," copy in Olustee Battlefield Museum, quoted in Bergeron, "The Battle of Olustee," 144.

17. James W. Grace to the editors, Feb. 25, 1864, in *New Bedford (MA) Mercury*, Mar. 9, 1864, in *On the Altar of Freedom: A Black Soldier's Civil War Letters from the Front*, ed. Virginia M. Adams (Amherst: University of Massachusetts Press, 1991), 114.

18. William H. Thomas to Theodore D. Jervey, July 30, 1911, Theodore D. Jervey Papers, South Carolina Historical Society, Charleston.

19. Cram to Mother, Aug. 9, 1864, in *Soldiering with Sherman: The Civil War Letters of George F. Cram*, ed. Jennifer Cain Bohrnstedt (DeKalb: Northern Illinois University Press, 2000), 133, quoted in John David Smith, "Let Us All Be Grateful That We Have Colored Troops That Will Fight," in Smith, *Black Soldiers in Blue*, 61.

20. Burnside testimony, Aug. 14, 1864, *OR*, ser. 1, vol. 40, part 1, p. 73, quoted in Smith, "Let Us All Be Grateful," 61.

21. Shurtleff in Charles B. Martin, "Jackson's Brigade in Battle of Nashville," *Confederate Veteran* 17 (Jan. 1909): 12, quoted in Versalle F. Washington, *Eagles on Their Buttons: A Black Infantry Regiment in the Civil War* (Columbia: University of Missouri Press, 1999), 53.

22. R. J. M. Blackett, ed., *Thomas Morris Chester, Black Civil War Correspondent: His Dispatches from the Virginia Front* (Baton Rouge: Louisiana State University Press, 1989), 153.

23. Martin, "Jackson's Brigade in Battle of Nashville," 12, quoted in James Lee McDonough, *Nashville: The Western Confederacy's Final Gamble* (Knoxville: University of Tennessee Press, 2004), 166.

24. *The Civil War Memoir of Philip Daingerfield Stephenson, D.D.*, ed. Nathaniel Cheairs Hughes Jr. (Conway: University of Central Arkansas Press, 1995), 320, quoted in McDonough, *Nashville*, 166.

25. Samuel Alonzo Cook Memoir, Tennessee State Library and Archives, Nashville, p. 7, quoted in McDonough, *Nashville*, 166–67.

26. Martin, "Jackson's Brigade in Battle of Nashville," 12, quoted in McDonough, *Nashville*, 167.

27. Edgar W. Jones, "History of the 18th Alabama Infantry," Alabama Department of Archives and History, Montgomery, 47, quoted in McDonough, *Nashville*, 231.

28. Col. Reuben D. Mussey to Capt. C. P. Brown, Dec. 21, 1864, in Letters Sent by the Commissioner, ser. 1141, Organization of U.S. Colored Troops, Dept. of the Cumberland; General Orders No. 5, HQ 100th Regt. U.S. Colored Infantry, Feb. 2, 1865, quoted in Berlin, *The Black Military Experience*, ser. 2, 561–63.

29. *OR*, ser. 1, vol. 15, p. 191, quoted in Ervin L. Jordan, *Black Confederates and Afro-Yankees in Civil War Virginia* (Charlottesville: University Press of Virginia, 1995), 273.

30. Civil War African-American Medal of Honor Recipients, www.buffalosoldier .net/civilwarafrican-americanmedalofhonorrecipients.htm, accessed Mar. 3, 2013.

31. Ibid.

32. William A. Dobak, *Freedom by the Sword: The U.S. Colored Troops, 1862–1867* (Washington, DC: U.S. Army Center of Military History, 2011), 499.

33. J. M. Addeman, *Reminiscences of Two Years with the Colored Troops* (Providence, RI: N. Bangs Williams, 1880), 36; "Shocking Occurrence at Sea: The Steamer Atlanta Breaks in Pieces and Sinks in Mid-Ocean," *New York Times*, Oct. 21, 1865, p. 2.

EPILOGUE

1. Gideon Welles, *Diary of Gideon Welles, Secretary of the Navy under Lincoln and Johnson*, 3 vols. (1909; reprint, New York: Houghton Mifflin, 1911), 2:293.

2. "The Last of Earth: The Solemn Funeral Ceremonies at Washington," *Chicago Tribune*, Apr. 20, 1865, p. 1.

3. Fleetwood to Dr. James Hall, June 8, 1865, www.nps.gov/rich/historyculture/ writings3.htm, accessed Mar. 3, 2013. The original of Fleetwood's letter resides in the Carter G. Woodson Collection, Manuscript Division, Library of Congress, Washington, DC.

SELECTED FURTHER READING

Determined to tell their story both to challenge white racism and to underscore black accomplishment, honor, and masculinity during the post–Civil War years, former slaves, free blacks, and white officers first chronicled the history of the U.S. Colored Troops.

As early as 1867 William Wells Brown, the renowned slave fugitive and black novelist, published *The Negro in the American Rebellion: His Heroism and His Fidelity* (1867; reprint, Athens: Ohio University Press, 2003), followed three years later by the classic *Army Life in a Black Regiment* (1870; reprint, New York: Penguin, 1997) by Thomas Wentworth Higginson, the white abolitionist and commander of the 1st South Carolina Volunteer Regiment. In 1887 George Washington Williams published *A History of the Negro Troops in the War of the Rebellion, 1861–1865* (1887; reprint, New York: Fordham University Press, 2012). Having fought in the 41st USCT and, later, in the famed 10th U.S. Cavalry, Williams emphasized the African American troops' martial prowess, judging it "not only the proud and priceless heritage of a race, but the glory of a nation." Coincidentally, in 1887 Joseph T. Wilson, another person of color who fought in two black Civil War regiments, published *The Black Phalanx: African American Soldiers in the War of Independence, the War of 1812, and the Civil War* (1887; reprint, New York: Da Capo, 1994), a work that framed the massacres of the men of the USCT at such battles as Fort Pillow within the racial violence rampant in the age of Jim Crow. Four years later Luis F. Emilio, a white officer in the 54th Massachusetts Volunteer Regiment, wrote *A Brave Black Regiment: The History of the 54th Massachusetts, 1863–1865* (1891; reprint, New York: Da Capo, 1995), a work historians still consider a valuable narrative of that famous unit.

The modern study of the USCT paralleled the rise of the post–World War II civil rights movement. It began with the publication of Benjamin Quarles's pathbreaking overview, *The Negro in the Civil War* (Boston: Little, Brown, 1953), and Dudley Taylor Cornish's detailed *The Sable Arm: Negro Troops in the Union Army, 1861–1865* (1956; reprint, Lawrence: University Press of Kansas, 1987). Both remain invaluable. Two other works—Quarles's *Lincoln and the Negro* (New York: Oxford University Press, 1962) and James M. McPherson's *The Negro's Civil War: How American Negroes Felt and Acted during the War for the Union* (1965; reprint, Urbana: University of Illinois Press, 1982)—continue to define the contours of later writing on the USCT. Perhaps the single most valuable work on the USCT remains Ira Berlin, ed., *Freedom: A*

Documentary History of Reconstruction, 1861–1867, ser. 2, *The Black Military Experience* (Cambridge: Cambridge University Press, 1982).

President Abraham Lincoln's racial views generally, and his emerging support of military emancipation and his mobilization of the USCT in particular, have attracted considerable scholarship. The best works include John Hope Franklin, *The Emancipation Proclamation* (Garden City, NY: Doubleday, 1963); Allen C. Guelzo, *Lincoln's Emancipation Proclamation: The End of Slavery in America* (New York: Simon and Schuster, 2004); Harold Holzer, Edna Greene Medford, and Frank J. Williams, *The Emancipation Proclamation: Three Views* (Baton Rouge: Louisiana State University Press, 2006); Paul D. Escott, *"What Shall We Do with the Negro?": Lincoln, White Racism, and Civil War America* (Charlottesville: University of Virginia Press, 2009); Henry Louis Gates Jr., ed., *Lincoln on Race and Slavery* (Princeton, NJ: Princeton University Press, 2009); William A. Blair and Karen Fisher Younger, eds., *Lincoln's Proclamation: Emancipation Reconsidered* (Chapel Hill: University of North Carolina Press, 2009); Eric Foner, *The Fiery Trial: Abraham Lincoln and American Slavery* (New York: W. W. Norton, 2010); Harold Holzer, *Emancipating Lincoln: The Proclamation in Text, Context, and Memory* (Cambridge, MA: Harvard University Press, 2012); Louis P. Masur, *Lincoln's Hundred Days: The Emancipation Proclamation and the War for the Union* (Cambridge, MA: Belknap Press of Harvard University Press, 2012); Brian R. Dirck, *Abraham Lincoln and White America* (Lawrence: University Press of Kansas, 2012); Richard Slotkin, *The Long Road to Antietam: How the Civil War Became a Revolution* (New York: Liveright, 2012); Bruce Levine, *The Fall of the House of Dixie: The Civil War and the Social Revolution That Transformed the South* (New York: Random House, 2013); James Oakes, *Freedom National: The Destruction of Slavery in the United States, 1861–1865* (New York: W. W. Norton, 2013); and John David Smith, *Lincoln and the U.S. Colored Troops* (Carbondale: Southern Illinois University Press, 2013).

Among recent studies of the USCT, Noah Andre Trudeau's *Like Men of War: Black Troops in the Civil War, 1862–1865* (Boston: Little, Brown, 1998) is an accurate, fast-paced, and highly readable military history. In *Freedom by the Sword: The U.S. Colored Troops, 1862–1867* (Washington, DC: U.S. Army Center of Military History, 2011), William A. Dobak provides a highly detailed operational study. Two collections of essays—Howard C. Westwood's *Black Troops, White Commanders, and Freedmen during the Civil War* (Carbondale: Southern Illinois University Press, 1992) and John David Smith, ed., *Black Soldiers in Blue: African American Troops in the Civil War Era* (Chapel Hill: University of North Carolina Press, 2002)—cover various topics associated with the USCT, their commanders, and their military campaigns.

The scholarship on the USCT includes many excellent works devoted to specialized topics. On the relationship between white officers and their black soldiers, see Joseph T. Glatthaar, *Forged in Battle: The Civil War Alliance of Black Soldiers and White Officers* (New York: Free Press, 1990), and Martin W. Öfele, *German-Speaking Officers in the United States Colored Troops, 1863–1867* (Gainesville: University Press of Florida, 2004). On the social aspects of the men of the USCT, consult Keith P. Wilson's *Campfires of Freedom: The Camp Life of Black Soldiers during the Civil War* (Kent, OH:

Kent State University Press, 2002). Chandra Manning's *What This Cruel War Was Over: Soldiers, Slavery, and the Civil War* (New York: Alfred A. Knopf, 2007) examines how rank-and-file Union and Confederates troops responded to the USCT.

For insights into the recruitment of USCT regiments, how white soldiers gained commissions in black units, and the black recruits' training, respectively, see *The Diary of James T. Ayres: Civil War Recruiter*, ed. John Hope Franklin (1947; reprint, Baton Rouge: Louisiana State University Press, 1999); *As If It Were Glory: Robert Beecham's Civil War from the Iron Brigade to the Black Regiments*, ed. Michael E. Stevens (Madison, WI: Madison House, 1998); and Donald Scott Sr., *Camp William Penn, 1863–1865* (Atglen, PA: Schiffer, 2012). Christian G. Samito provides an excellent account of the USCT's experience with military justice in *Becoming American under Fire: Irish Americans, African Americans, and the Politics of Citizenship during the Civil War* (Ithaca, NY: Cornell University Press, 2009). For firsthand accounts of the USCT's service on the James River front by an African American journalist, see R. J. M. Blackett, ed., *Thomas Morris Chester: Black Civil War Correspondent, His Dispatches from the Virginia Front* (Baton Rouge: Louisiana State University Press, 1989).

Contemporary scholars have begun researching individual USCT regiments. Their works include Edward A. Miller Jr., *The Black Civil War Soldiers of Illinois: The Story of the Twenty-Ninth U.S. Colored Infantry* (Columbia: University of South Carolina Press, 1998); James M. Paradis, *Strike the Blow for Freedom: The 6th United States Colored Infantry in the Civil War* (Shippensburg, PA: White Mane Books, 1998); Versalle F. Washington, *Eagles on Their Buttons: A Black Infantry Regiment in the Civil War* (Columbia: University of Missouri Press, 1999); Russell Duncan, *Where Death and Glory Meet: Colonel Robert Gould Shaw and the 54th Massachusetts Infantry* (Athens: University of Georgia Press, 1999); Martin H. Blatt, Thomas J. Brown, and Donald Yacovone, eds., *Hope & Glory: Essays on the Legacy of the 54th Massachusetts Regiment* (Amherst: University of Massachusetts Press, 2001); Edward G. Longacre, *A Regiment of Slaves: The 4th United States Colored Infantry, 1863–1866* (Mechanicsburg, PA: Stackpole Books, 2003); Stephen V. Ash, *Firebrand of Liberty: The Story of Two Black Regiments That Changed the Course of the Civil War* (New York: W. W. Norton, 2008); Richard M. Reid, *Freedom for Themselves: North Carolina's Black Soldiers in the Civil War Era* (Chapel Hill: University of North Carolina Press, 2008); and James K. Bryant II, *The 36th Infantry United States Colored Troops in the Civil War: A History and Roster* (Jefferson, NC: McFarland, 2012). On the Louisiana Native Guards, see James G. Hollandsworth Jr., *The Louisiana Native Guards: The Black Military Experience during the Civil War* (Baton Rouge: Louisiana State University Press, 1995); C. P. Weaver, ed., *Thank God My Regiment an African One: The Civil War Diary of Colonel Nathan W. Daniels* (Baton Rouge: Louisiana State University Press, 1998); and Stephen J. Ochs, *A Black Patriot and a White Priest: André Cailloux and Claude Paschal Maistre in Civil War New Orleans* (Baton Rouge: Louisiana State University Press, 2000).

Students will find useful histories of the medical care and condition of the men of the USCT in Margaret Humphreys, *Intensely Human: The Health of the Black Soldier in the American Civil War* (Baltimore: Johns Hopkins University Press, 2008); Richard M.

Reid, ed., *Practicing Medicine in a Black Regiment: The Civil War Diary of Burt G. Wilder, 55th Massachusetts* (Amherst: University of Massachusetts Press, 2010); and Jim Downs, *Sick from Freedom: African-American Illness and Suffering during the Civil War and Reconstruction* (New York: Oxford University Press, 2012). Susie King Taylor, *Reminiscences of My Life in Camp: An African American Woman's Civil War Memoir* (1902; reprint, Athens: University of Georgia Press, 2006), is a classic work that provides first-person insights into a nurse who succored men of the USCT.

The Confederates' response to the USCT, especially their refusal to take black prisoners of war, continues to attract high-quality scholarship. See Richard L. Fuchs, *An Unerring Fire: The Massacre at Fort Pillow* (Rutherford, NJ: Fairleigh Dickinson University Press, 1994); Thomas D. Mays, *The Saltville Massacre* (Fort Worth, TX: Ryan Place, 1995); John Cimprich, *Fort Pillow: A Civil War Massacre and Public Memory* (Baton Rouge: Louisiana State University Press, 2005); Gregory J. W. Urwin, ed., *Black Flag over Dixie: Racial Atrocities and Reprisals in the Civil War* (Carbondale: Southern Illinois University Press, 2004); Andrew Ward, *River Run Red: The Fort Pillow Massacre in the American Civil War* (New York: Viking, 2005); George S. Burkhardt, *Confederate Rage, Yankee Wrath: No Quarter in the Civil War* (Carbondale: Southern Illinois University Press, 2007); and Richard Slotkin, *No Quarter: The Battle of the Crater, 1864* (New York: Random House, 2009).

On African Americans in the Civil War–era U.S. Navy, see Steven J. Ramold, *Slaves, Sailors, Citizens: African Americans in the Union Navy* (DeKalb: Northern Illinois University Press, 2002); William B. Gould IV, ed., *Diary of a Contraband: The Civil War Passage of a Black Sailor* (Stanford, CA: Stanford University Press, 2002); Michael J. Bennett, *Union Jacks: Yankee Sailors in the Civil War* (Chapel Hill: University of North Carolina Press, 2004); and Barbara Brooks Tomblin, *Bluejackets and Contrabands: African Americans and the Union Navy* (Lexington: University Press of Kentucky, 2009).

Invaluable works on USCT veterans are Donald R. Shafer, *After the Glory: The Struggle of Black Civil War Veterans* (Lawrence: University Press of Kansas, 2004); Elizabeth A. Regosin and Donald R. Shafer, *Voices of Emancipation: Understanding Slavery, the Civil War, and Reconstruction through the U.S. Pension Files* (New York: New York University Press, 2008); and Barbara A. Gannon, *The Won Cause: Black and White Comradeship in the Grand Army of the Republic* (Chapel Hill: University of North Carolina Press, 2011). On African American soldiers after Appomattox, see James N. Leiker, *Racial Borders: Black Soldiers along the Rio Grande* (College Station: Texas A&M University Press, 2002); and Elizabeth D. Leonard, *Men of Color to Arms! Black Soldiers, Indian Wars, and the Quest for Equality* (New York: W. W. Norton, 2010).

Ronald S. Coddington's *African American Faces of the Civil War: An Album* (Baltimore: Johns Hopkins University Press, 2012) provides superb photographs of men of the USCT and insightful pen portraits. For the remarkable story of an escaped slave who spied for the Union army in Virginia, North Carolina, and the Mississippi River Valley and then recruited fugitive slaves for the USCT, see David S. Cecelski, *The Fire of Freedom: Abraham Galloway and the Slaves' Civil War* (Chapel Hill: University of North Carolina Press, 2012). Recent works that document ex-slaves' voices on emancipation, the USCT, and Reconstruction include Herbert C. Covey and Dwight Eisnach, *How the Slaves Saw the Civil War: Recollections of the War through the WPA Slave Narratives* (Santa Barbara, CA: Praeger/ABC-CLIO, 2014), and John David Smith, *We Ask Only for Even-Handed Justice: Black Voices from Reconstruction, 1865–1877* (Amherst: University of Massachusetts Press, 2014).

INDEX

Page numbers in italics refer to illustrations.